Cambridge Elements ☰

Elements in Epistemology
edited by
Stephen Hetherington
University of New South Wales, Sydney

TRANSCENDENTAL EPISTEMOLOGY

Tony Cheng
National Chengchi University and Waseda University

CAMBRIDGE
UNIVERSITY PRESS

Shaftesbury Road, Cambridge CB2 8EA, United Kingdom

One Liberty Plaza, 20th Floor, New York, NY 10006, USA

477 Williamstown Road, Port Melbourne, VIC 3207, Australia

314–321, 3rd Floor, Plot 3, Splendor Forum, Jasola District Centre,
New Delhi – 110025, India

103 Penang Road, #05–06/07, Visioncrest Commercial, Singapore 238467

Cambridge University Press is part of Cambridge University Press & Assessment,
a department of the University of Cambridge.

We share the University's mission to contribute to society through the pursuit of
education, learning and research at the highest international levels of excellence.

www.cambridge.org
Information on this title: www.cambridge.org/9781009478632

DOI: 10.1017/9781009243834

First published 2024

A catalogue record for this publication is available from the British Library.

ISBN 978-1-009-47863-2 Hardback
ISBN 978-1-009-24382-7 Paperback
ISSN 2398-0567 (online)
ISSN 2514-3832 (print)

Cambridge University Press & Assessment has no responsibility for the persistence
or accuracy of URLs for external or third-party internet websites referred to in this
publication and does not guarantee that any content on such websites is, or will
remain, accurate or appropriate.

Transcendental Epistemology

Elements in Epistemology

DOI: 10.1017/9781009243834
First published online: January 2024

Tony Cheng
National Chengchi University and Waseda University
Author for correspondence: Tony Cheng, h.cheng.12@ucl.ac.uk

Abstract: Transcendental arguments were once very prominent in Western philosophy, notably in German idealism, the phenomenological tradition, and P. F. Strawson's thinking. However, they have fallen out of fashion because of their associations with transcendental idealism and verificationism. Somewhat paradoxically, they are still often invoked by important figures in the analytic tradition, even if the very same tradition has cast much doubt on such arguments. Even more problematically, the nature of transcendental arguments remains unclear: are they supposed to be deductive? Are they synthetic or analytic? If they are a priori, how are they supposed to be about the empirical world? What are their relations to necessity, conceivability, and essence? This Element takes up the challenge of elucidating the nature of transcendental arguments, as embedded in the wider context of transcendental epistemology. It will be argued that the key premise – known as 'transcendental conditional' – might be synthetic, necessary, and a posteriori.

This Element also has a video abstract: www.cambridge.org/cheng

Keywords: epistemology, transcendental arguments, how-possible questions, modality, possibilitation

ISBNs: 9781009478632 (HB), 9781009243827 (PB), 9781009243834 (OC)
ISSNs: 2398-0567 (online), 2514-3832 (print)

Contents

1 Transcendental Epistemology Introduced — 1

2 What Are Transcendental Arguments? The History
Overviewed — 16

3 What Should Transcendental Arguments Be?
A Hypothesis Proposed — 31

4 Transcendental Arguments in Action: The Revisionary
Hypothesis Applied — 42

5 Roads Ahead — 51

References — 62

1 Transcendental Epistemology Introduced

This Element is entitled *Transcendental Epistemology*, but the main bulk of it is on the so-called transcendental argument. This implies a philosophical outlook that the author is recommending, but it is a controversial one, just like other outlooks in philosophy. In order to find this narrative intelligible, some stage settings are required.

First of all, what is epistemology? Etymology aside, in general it refers to the part of philosophy that is about the study of how we *know* things, or the theory of knowledge, especially with regard to its methods, validity, and scope, and to the distinction between *justified* belief and opinion. If one looks into various branches of epistemology, one would presumably discover two groups, as follows:

Group 1: Approaches – virtue epistemology; formal epistemology; scientific epistemology.

Group 2: Domains – moral epistemology; modal epistemology; social epistemology; epistemology of science.

The list is far from exhaustive, but it is enough to illustrate the crucial point that can help us understand what transcendental epistemology is. To begin with, branches of epistemology can be about specific *approaches* to standard questions in epistemology. For example, virtue epistemology aims to solve standard questions with certain notions of *virtue* (Sosa 2007); formal epistemology seeks to tackle standard questions with *formal* methods from mathematics and logic (Bradley 2015),; and scientific epistemology attempts to approach standard questions with *scientifically* informed methods (Kornblith 2021). By contrast, other branches of epistemology can be about specific *domains* in epistemology. For example, moral epistemology discusses how we know about *moral* truths, if there are any (Zimmerman 2010). Modal epistemology studies how we know about *modal* truths, if there are any (Mallozzi, Vaidya, and Wallner 2021). Epistemology of science is also a branch of philosophy of science, asking how we go about gaining *scientific* knowledge (Bird 2010). This contrast, to be sure, is not completely sharp, but it is a rough-and-ready one that helps us understand what a branch of epistemology is about when we encounter a new label. Now what about *transcendental epistemology*? Is it an approach or a domain? Interestingly, it seems to be both. When one invokes transcendental arguments or methods (to be defined) to support certain conclusions, the emphasis is more on the *approach*, while when we focus on a specific kind of 'how-possible' question, the emphasis is more on the *domain*. We will focus on the domain reading here, as it is more controversial given Cassam's (2007) criticisms. As for the approach reading, it is actually quite straightforward: one can invoke transcendental arguments to support conclusions in ethics, metaphysics, philosophy of perception, and so on. Whether such arguments are effective, to be sure, is a matter that needs to be dealt with in a case-by-case manner, in addition to the general considerations we will examine.

'Transcendental epistemology' is a rare label; it is almost non-existent compared to 'virtue epistemology' or 'modal epistemology'. What is transcendental epistemology, exactly? According to its most prominent contemporary advocate, Quassim Cassam: 'Transcendental epistemology is, among other things, an inquiry into the conditions of human knowledge. The conditions which are the focus of transcendental epistemology are *transcendentally necessary* conditions, that is, necessary conditions which "reflect the structure of the human cognitive apparatus"' (Cassam 2003: 181, referring to Allison 1983; see also Cassam 1998).

Later, I will argue that the characterisation here is good though incomplete, but for ease of exposition, let's stick to it for now.[1] Later in his seminal work *The Possibility of Knowledge*, Cassam (2007) investigates a specific kind of 'how-possible' question, and proposes his own 'multi-levels response' to such questions. This is a prime example of transcendental epistemology. We will have a brief look at Cassam's framework in Sections 1.1 and 1.2, and introduce our alternative later. But before that, at the very beginning of this Element, I shall provide a more general background to motivate this investigation. After all, the very facts that 'transcendental epistemology' is a rare label and (relatedly) that 'transcendental arguments' are often relegated to a corner of history might indicate that most of us should not bother with them. Let me briefly counter this impression here. Parts of what I am now going to say will be slightly repetitive with some later content, but in order to motivate this investigation for the general audience, some anticipations are called for.[2]

The first obvious thing here is that many big names have been said to invoke such arguments, including Aristotle, Descartes, Kant, Fichte, Hegel, Wittgenstein, Davidson, Strawson, Putnam, Evans, Korsgaard, McDowell, and so on. Isn't this enough to show we should care? Perhaps not, one might contend: what if one works on a kind of philosophy which is simply *not* relevant to these names? Or what if one works on Aristotle but simply does not touch on the relevant bit, that is, the alleged transcendental argument for non-contradiction? It seems that this first reason by itself is not strong enough.

---

[1] To anticipate, it will be argued that the conditions not only reflect the structure of human cognitive apparatus, but also *possibilitate* the target phenomenon.

[2] The editor and one reviewer of this Element have emphasised the importance of stage setting here.

Another reason is not only that many big names have been said to invoke such arguments, but also that many central topics unavoidably involve transcendental reasonings. For example, issues concerning values, free will, scepticism, semantic meanings, objectivity, time, to name just a few, have bearings with such arguments. Of course, it is always possible to work on those areas without worrying about transcendental arguments, but if they are ubiquitous, it becomes arbitrary or even intellectually irresponsible to ignore them.

Now, the above two reasons, even if good, are about transcendental *arguments*. What about transcendental *epistemology*, or more broadly, transcendental *philosophy*? Isn't it the case that one can work on ethics, metaphysics, or epistemology without touching on this Kantian branch? To satisfactorily answer this challenge will take us to Section 1.1 and beyond, since the key here is that transcendental philosophy centres on a kind of how-possible question, which will be explained in the following sections. For now, we need to only focus on this point: many fundamental questions in philosophy are about the *nature* of things. For example, What is goodness? What is free will? What is knowledge? Upon reflection, these kinds of questions presuppose corresponding transcendental questions, which are about the *possibility* of those things:

1. 'What is goodness?' To answer this, we need to confront a conceptually prior question, 'how is goodness possible, given that individual creatures are selfish?'.
2. 'What is free will?' To answer this, we need to confront a conceptually prior question, 'how is free will possible, given determinism or quantum mechanics?'.
3. 'What is knowledge?' To answer this, we need to confront a conceptually prior question, 'how is knowledge possible, given evil demon or dream scepticism?'.

To fully appreciate the significance of this third reason, we need to look into the subject matter discussed in the follow sections. The main message of this introductory section is that transcendental arguments, transcendental epistemology (both as an approach and as a domain), and transcendental philosophy are *not* parochial or obsolete areas of philosophy. Rather, they occupy central parts of philosophy in the past, the present, and the future.

1.1 Epistemological How-Possible Questions

Not all how-possible questions are philosophically interesting. In sports, we ask how it is possible for certain players to achieve certain levels of performance. In such circumstances, we ask such questions because we feel that those performances are incredible, but there is nothing *logically, metaphysically,* or even *physically* impossible about them. However incredible they are, such performances do not violate physical laws. Philosophically interesting how-possible questions are *not* like that. Here is how Cassam introduces the subject matter: 'How-possible questions matter in philosophy because, as Nozick points out, "many philosophical problems are ones of understanding how something is or can be possible" ([Nozick]1981: 8) … how-possible questions are *obstacle-dependent* questions. We ask how x is possible when there appears to be an obstacle to the existence of x' (Cassam 2007: 1–2).

The idea is this: how-possible questions in philosophy make sense when we ask how *x* is possible *given* certain views we hold true. For example, how is freedom of the will possible, *given* determinism? One can of course reject determinism, but the challenge can be refined: how is freedom of the will possible, *given* that the world is either deterministic or indeterministic, but neither of them seems to fit our idea of freedom? Cassam points out that there are two basic strategies: 'The first is to deny the existence of the obstacle which gave rise to the question. This is an *obstacle-dissipating* strategy … [other ways] are *obstacle-overcoming* rather than obstacle-dissipating strategies since they don't straightforwardly deny the existence of the obstacle … What they deny is that the alleged obstacles are insuperable and, in this sense, genuine' (Cassam 2007: 2).

We will say more about this in Section 1.2. Now, there is actually a third strategy, that is, scepticism, which denies that the obstacles in question can either be dissipated or overcome. For our purposes, scepticism will be mostly in the background, but the existence of this option reminds us of the relevance of epistemology in asking philosophically significant how-possible questions.

How-possible questions in this sense can be said to define *transcendental philosophy,* but do not yet define *transcendental epistemology* as a domain. As Cassam (2007: 3) says, his 'concern is with epistemological rather than metaphysical, ethical, or theological how-possible questions'. So, for transcendental epistemology, the key questions are *epistemological* how-possible questions. Prominent topics include perceptual knowledge, knowledge of other minds, and a priori knowledge. In this Element, we will not focus on these questions per se. Rather, we will compare Cassam's multi-levels response and the traditional response based on transcendental arguments (in the rest of Section 1). We will next provide some historical overviews of transcendental arguments in the history of Western philosophy (Section 2), and propose a new way of putting transcendental arguments to work (Section 3). We will then use this new way to look at three examples of transcendental arguments in epistemology (Section 4) and, finally, discuss prominent questions concerning naturalisation, explanation, and scepticism (Section 5). It is likely that readers will not find the hypothesis put forward in Section 3 convincing, but even if that hypothesis turns out to be false, this intellectual journey will still teach us much about transcendental epistemology, both as an approach and a domain, and the relevant parts of history of philosophy.

1.2 Cassam's Multi-Levels Response

Invoking transcendental arguments has been the traditional approach when tackling how-possible questions in the relevant sense, and that will be our main topic in the rest of this Element. Before going into these details, it is essential to look into a recent alternative in Cassam (2007), as indicated in the previous section. Cassam argues that his multi-levels response is superior to transcendental arguments. In this section we will discuss the gist of his alternative.

To begin with, note that, strictly speaking, the contrast between a multi-levels response and transcendental arguments is not exactly correct: obviously, if one side is 'multi-levels', the opposing side should be 'single-level'. That might indeed be one way of setting up the dialectic: as Cassam points out, some might think that transcendental arguments are themselves *sufficient* for responding to the relevant how-possible questions. However, Cassam thinks that is not the most sensible way of defending the role of transcendental arguments in this context, as we shall see. But to understand this, we need to have a basic grasp of Cassam's multi-levels response.

Cassam's characterisations of and arguments for his proposal are very rich and intricate; in what follows we only provide a sketch of them. Again, here is how he introduces the relevant kind of how-possible question: 'To ask a how-possible question is to ask how something which looks impossible given other things that one knows or believes is nevertheless possible' (Cassam 2007: 1, with a reference to Dray 1957).

Prominent examples in philosophy include 'How is freedom of the will possible, given determinism?' and 'How is evil possible, given certain views about God?'. From these examples, we can see that 'how-possible questions are *obstacle-dependent* questions' (Cassam 2007: 2; original italics). The relevant obstacles, or at least apparent obstacles, make it intelligible to ask those how-possible questions. What do we do about those obstacles? There are two main strategies:

Obstacles-dissipating strategy: to 'deny the existence of the obstacle' (Cassam 2007: 2).

Obstacle-overcoming strategy: to deny that 'the alleged obstacles are insuperable and, in this sense, genuine' (Cassam 2007: 2).

Now why is Cassam's proposal a 'multi-levels response'? Let's see what those levels are:

> Level 1, Means: The level at which means of knowing about a certain subject matter are identified.
>
> Level 2, Obstacle Removement: The level at which obstacles to the acquisition of knowledge by the proposed means are overcome or dissipated.
>
> Level 3, Enabling Conditions: The level at which enabling conditions for knowing by the proposed means are identified. (Cassam 2007: 9–10)

And there is a further contrast:

> Minimalism: One should stop at level 2.
> Moderate Anti-Minimalism: One *can* continue to level 3.
> Extreme Anti-Minimalism: One *should* continue to level 3. (Cassam 2007: 10 and sect. 1.4)

This is the general shape of Cassam's framework. In Cassam (2007) he interprets Kant as holding extreme anti-minimalism and argues against it. Cassam himself holds moderate anti-minimalism. For our purposes, we will focus on his discussions of level 3, as it is where he touches on transcendental arguments. First, we will describe how he understands this level, then we will evaluate his idea that transcendental arguments, though they look similar to this level, are nevertheless *irrelevant* when it comes to the kind of how-possible questions we care about. Finally, we will explain why, properly understood, transcendental arguments *can* still be regarded as useful in this context, contra Cassam. We will need to leave the latter two points until the end of Section 1.3.

How does Cassam understand level 3? To answer this question, we need to look into how he understands *enabling conditions*. Instead of giving a single definition, Cassam gives various characterisations in different contexts. When it comes to the possibility of perceptual knowledge, the relevant enabling conditions are 'the conditions under which it is possible for perception to be a source of knowledge of the things around us' (Cassam 2007: 9). From this we can see that the enabling conditions need to be coupled with specific means (e.g., perception in this case) as a source of the knowledge in question. However, in this description Cassam does not explicitly state what he means by 'enabling'. He does have much more to say about it though; consider this passage: 'What are enabling conditions? In essence, they are a sub-class of necessary conditions ... [they] are necessary conditions for achieving something by a particular means. Relatedly, enabling conditions are *background* conditions, which may or may not be causal'(Cassam 2007: 17; original italics).

But what do we mean by 'background' here? Cassam invokes a common example to cash it out:

> Being an unmarried man is a necessary condition for being a bachelor but being an unmarried man isn't an enabling condition for being a bachelor. Intuitively, the reason is that being an unmarried man isn't a 'background condition' for being a bachelor. Being an unmarried man doesn't just 'enable' one to be a bachelor, it is what being a bachelor consists in. (Cassam 2007: 17)

The two passages just quoted generate lots of questions. I discuss some of them below:

1. Why are enabling conditions *necessary* conditions at all? Note that Cassam says that these conditions may or may not be *causal*. If they are non-causal, they might be a priori, so it is natural to expect that they are necessary. But in that case, how can they be necessary conditions for achieving something by a particular means? After all, 'achievement' in this context does sound causal. Now, if they are causal, it is at least controversial to hold that they are necessary, for Humean reasons. Cassam mentions that 'Dretske and Searle take it that enabling conditions are causally necessary conditions' (Cassam 2007: 17), so we know that they opt for a non-Humean picture, which is not a problem as such.[3]
2. In what sense are these conditions *enabling* ones? Presumably, being an unmarried man does not enable one to be a bachelor *at all*. More accurately, being an unmarried man *semantically entails* being a bachelor. Whether this fits Cassam's 'consists in' expression depends on how we understand that notion. This might be fine, but it also leads to our next point.
3. In what sense are these conditions *background* ones? Cassam's remark that being an unmarried man isn't a 'background condition' for being a bachelor gives us some clues by elimination. But without a more explicit character-isation of what background conditions are, we cannot know more about the positive picture.

In the remainder of this section, I will argue that Cassam's reliance on the notions, or at least the expressions of, 'enabling conditions' and 'background conditions' is misplaced, although this does not really threaten his positive proposal directly. To begin with, it is illuminating to see how terms such as 'enabling conditions' and 'background conditions' are used in the literature.

---

[3] Based on Mackie (1965), Cassam (personal communications) expresses concerns about my interpretation of the Humean picture here, but I shall not go into exegetic issues in this context. Also, he reminds that background conditions here might be related to John Searle's (1983) notion of 'background' in *Intentionality* (and Tyler Burge's (1996) discussion of entitlement to self-knowledge, but the relation is too vague to be stated precisely here).

In his comment on Daniel Dennett's (1978) overall picture, John McDowell (1994) invokes the distinction between *enabling* explanations and *constitutive* explanations. This corresponds to two other distinctions: the one between the subpersonal and the personal, and the one between cognitive sciences and philosophy. It is arguable that this mapping of the three distinctions is controversial (Hornsby 1981; Drayson 2012), but what we need here is not such a mapping. What should be taken seriously is the one between the enabling and the constitutive: while the former is about the *causal mechanisms* underpinning the relevant phenomenon, the latter is about the *nature* of such a phenomenon. Now, how does this compare to Cassam's usage? Recall that for him, enabling conditions may or may not be causal, but that seems to be too broad a notion in this context. Whether something is causally efficacious seems to be a feature that carves nature at its joints; of course, we can have a category which encompasses a causal and a non-causal variant, but given that the natural reading of 'enabling' is causal, as can be seen in the McDowell–Dennett exchange, 'enabling conditions' is not the best term for Cassam's purposes.[4]

What about 'background conditions'? The natural contrast with 'background' should be 'foreground' or similar notions, but it is unclear why Cassam's level 3 involves anything like background conditions if we have this contrast in mind. Here it is illuminating to see how 'background conditions' are used in the literature on the neural correlates of consciousness (NCCs). Let's suppose that V1 to V4 and certain parts of the prefrontal cortex are jointly responsible for visual consciousness. If that is so, it is apt to say that certain activities in V1 to V4 and certain parts of the prefrontal cortex are the enabling conditions of visual consciousness. They are *in the foreground*, as it were. What are the relevant *background* conditions? Well, other parts of the brain need to function appropriately; the organism needs to be alive; and in order for that to happen, the environment needs to have enough oxygen, water, and so on. The difficult question in this area is where to draw the exact line between the NCCs and the supporting elements, that is, the foregrounds and the backgrounds. However, in order to grasp this distinction, we do not need to settle this theoretical question. Suffice to emphasise that in order to make sense of the backgrounds, we need to have a clear contrast of foregrounds, but it is unclear what the contrast is in Cassam's picture.

Now, one might argue on Cassam's behalf that these are all terms of art, and the fact that 'enabling conditions' and 'background conditions' are used differently by others does not mean that Cassam cannot use those terms in his way.

---

[4] For more on this with a phenomenological twist, see Wheeler (2013), who aims to reconcile transcendental phenomenology and cognitive sciences. I thank a reviewer for pointing this out.

Fair enough. The point here is not that Cassam cannot use those terms in his way; it is rather that his way of using the terms is misleading, and is not the best way to convey his good points. To reprise, enabling conditions are more naturally understood as causal mechanisms, while background conditions are more naturally understood as contrasting with foreground conditions. Both are different from Cassam's usage. We have no right to demand that those who side with Cassam should change their preferred way, but here we propose that both 'enabling conditions' and 'background conditions' are no good in this context.

What then? Suppose that we tentatively agree with the negative points cited. What can we say positively about the conditions? In Section 3.3, we will introduce a notion of 'possibilitation' for this specific purpose; it is neither enabling nor background conditions. For now, we can stick to Cassam's original proposal, without using his terminologies. For Cassam, level 3 asks 'what-makes-it-possible questions' that are 'explanation-seeking' (Cassam 2007: 16; see also McDowell 1998). We will follow this route, but with two points of disagreement: first, 'background enabling conditions' are not what we need here; second, and more importantly, this level should be able to be fulfilled with the help of *transcendental arguments*. We have argued for the first point. For the second point, we will need to see what, roughly, transcendental arguments are, why Cassam thinks that transcendental arguments cannot fit the bill, and how we can respond to his concerns. This will take us to the centre of transcendental philosophy.

1.3 Transcendental Arguments, First Pass

The rest of this Element will be largely about transcendental arguments, but we have not said what they are. For Cassam, at least after 2007, transcendental epistemology can and perhaps should do without transcendental arguments. By contrast, our hypothesis is that transcendental arguments, properly understood, should be an integral part of transcendental epistemology (as a domain). Before saying more about Cassam's perspective, and how we can respond to that, we need to have a look at the general shape of transcendental arguments.

This section will only scratch the surface of that general shape. Section 2 will cover some transcendental arguments in Kant, German idealism, phenomenology, and analytic philosophy. And then Section 3 will be about how transcendental arguments, or at least some of them, should be understood in order for them to be plausible. In this section we will not dig into those areas; instead, we will survey how the contemporary literature understands transcendental arguments.

It is helpful to begin with general introductions to transcendental arguments, such as the relevant entries in the *Stanford Encyclopedia of Philosophy*

(SEP) and the *Internet Encyclopedia of Philosophy* (IEP). The former charac-
terises them in the following way: 'As standardly conceived, transcendental
arguments are taken to be distinctive in involving a certain sort of claim,
namely that X is a necessary condition for the possibility of Y – where then,
given that Y is the case, it logically follows that X must be the case'(Stern and
Cheng 2023).

This characterisation, though indeed standard, raises a number of issues. How
many claims are there in one transcendental argument? What is the difference
between such arguments and standard *modus ponens*? Must transcendental
arguments be logically deductive? How many modalities are involved in
them? Let's partially answer these questions.[5]

To begin with, according to the passage quoted, such an argument involves at
least two claims as premises: (1) he possibility of Y requires or presupposes X; and
(2) Y is the case. Several comments are in order. To begin with, this is indeed
similar to *modus ponens*, except that the antecedent of the conditional involves
a modal. Relatedly, here it looks like it is supposed to be logically deductive, but as
we shall see in Section 2, this was not always the case in a large part of the history
of transcendental arguments. How many modalities are involved here? It is not so
clear. It seems that we have 'the possibility' in the antecedent, and the conclusion
that X 'must' be the case. How about 'necessary conditions'? In contemporary
modal logic, we do not invoke a 'box' to formalise it, but this does not mean that it
is not a modal. We leave these questions open at this point. The crucial message
here is that they seem obvious and important, but surprisingly, they are not dealt
with explicitly in the contemporary literature of transcendental arguments. This is
not in itself a criticism, but it is noticeable that there are many questions
unanswered or even unrecognised so far.

Now let's check the entry from IEP: 'Transcendental arguments are partly
non-empirical often anti-skeptical arguments focusing on necessary enabling
conditions either of coherent experience or the possession or employment of
some kind of knowledge or cognitive ability, where the opponent is not in
a position to question the fact of this experience, knowledge, or cognitive
ability, and where the revealed preconditions include what the opponent
questions'(Bardon 2006).

Before analysing the passage, note that it does not speak to the questions I have
just raised, and this further confirms my claim that they are not considered
explicitly in the contemporary literature. Now what about this passage itself?

---

[5] Even deductive inferences based on *modus ponens* can involve difficult issues (Boghossian 2003;
Williamson 2003), but we leave that aside.

By 'partly non-empirical' it might mean that part of the argument is a priori. If the standard transcendental argument involves two claims, and one of them is a conditional, it is often thought that the conditional itself is a priori (for a recent example, see Schwenkler 2012). This will be challenged later in Section 3. As for the 'anti-sceptical' character, it is indeed one of the key features of transcendental arguments, but we will leave it to later discussions. The reason is that anti-scepticism seems to be overemphasised in the recent literature, and in what follows we will take the view that although anti-scepticism is indeed an *important* feature of transcendental arguments, it is *far from essential*, and it should not be taken as the core of such arguments.

The next rather interesting point is the mention of 'necessary enabling conditions', but nowhere in the passage is what we should mean by 'enabling' explained. Therefore, we stick to the point already made that 'enabling' terminology should be avoided altogether. The phrase 'coherent experience or the possession or employment of some kind of knowledge or cognitive ability' concerns the other premise, the one other than the conditional. It is supposed to affirm the antecedent: since coherent experience is actual, it is ipso facto possible, so the consequent of the conditional can be affirmed too. At this point, one wishes to know not only how transcendental arguments are different from standard *modus ponens*, but also why we need a modal claim to begin with: doesn't that further complicate things? Again, we leave these doubts open for now. They will be clarified in due course, especially by way of understanding the history of transcendental arguments: since such arguments have roots from hundreds of years ago, our discussions of them have to be historically informed, at least to some extent. This will be the task of the next section. Only after we have had some discussion of Kant, for example, can we see why Cassam holds that transcendental arguments cannot be the level 3 story, and how we can respond to his critical points. In the remainder of this section, we will say a bit more about how transcendental arguments are understood nowadays, according to the canonical characterisations of Stern and Cheng (2023). We will focus on critical engagements with the main ideas (for a full description of those features, see the SEP entry (Stern and Cheng 2023)).[6]

1. 'Transcendental arguments are anti-sceptical' (Stern and Cheng 2023).
    This is indeed a key feature that one always sees in the relevant literature, but is it an essential one? It is not so clear. Suppose that we take two paradigms from Kant's *Critique of Pure Reason*: the Transcendental Deduction and the

---

[6] It might seem a bit strange that I am responding to a piece which I co-authored, but that is because in Stern and Cheng (2023) we mostly follow Stern's original version. My main contribution there is on the relevance of modal metaphysics and epistemology (section 5), and on examples of transcendental arguments in philosophy of psychology and perception. These are not directly touched on in this context (section 7).

Refutation of Idealism (we will come back to these in Section 2). The latter is blatantly an attempted refutation of Cartesian scepticism, while the former is not too clear. Stern and Cheng (2023) write that 'the Deduction is directed against Humean scepticism concerning the applicability of a priori concepts to our experience'. But this is based on a very broad understanding of scepticism: for any thesis, there is a potential antithesis, and according to this usage, since Kant holds that a priori concepts are applicable to our experience, those who are against this automatically become sceptics. But this is not how we normally understand 'scepticism' in philosophy. Consider a contemporary example: that the possibility of intentionality requires or presupposes strong conceptualism, the view that experiences have representational contents and *all* of those contents are conceptual (McDowell 1996; more on this in Section 4). If we adopt this usage, then weak conceptualism (Peacocke 1992) and non-conceptualism (Evans 1982) automatically become versions of scepticism, but this is clearly a wrong verdict. True, one can say that Peacocke and Evans are sceptical about McDowell's view, but that fits our everyday usage of the term 'being sceptical'. When it comes to the noun 'scepticism' in philosophy, it refers to specific views, be it scepticism about the external world, other minds, moral values, and so on. Therefore, we should say that being anti-sceptical is a common feature that can be seen in many transcendental arguments, but the further claim that it is an *essential* feature should be resisted. We will come back to this in Section 5.3.

2. 'Because of this anti-sceptical purpose, transcendental arguments must begin from a starting point the relevant sceptic can be expected to accept. And given this, transcendental arguments will also characteristically be first personal' (Stern and Cheng 2023).

Having cast doubt about anti-scepticism being essential to transcendental arguments, we should still insist that *many* transcendental arguments are anti-sceptical in character. Now, *must* they begin from a starting point the relevant sceptic can be expected to accept? This seems exactly correct. And is it the case that given this, transcendental arguments will also *characteristically* be first personal? This seems exactly correct too. The Stern and Cheng (2023) entry is careful in making the two claims with different strengths: it is true that in order to ensure that the sceptics would accept the starting point, it is a *must* that those sceptics can be expected to accept those points. And it is also true that these arguments will also *characteristically* be first personal in the sense that the starting points are often variants of conscious experiences, as we shall see in the following sections. Still, it is crucial to emphasise that it is only characteristic, not necessary, that these starting points involve something first personal. We should leave open the possibility that in specific contexts the relevant sceptics can accept certain starting points that are *not* first personal. It might be difficult to come up with clear examples (but see Section 2.1 for the example from Aristotle), but there is no principled reason to restrict the starting points to first personal phenomena.

3. 'The necessity in transcendental arguments cannot be causal or natural necessity. It is instead metaphysical necessity or involves synthetic a priori statements' (Stern and Cheng 2023).

   This will actually be our focal disagreement throughout the Element, and full discussions will be carried out in later sections, but it will be illuminating if we anticipate the main points here. Let's begin with the negative part. Many writers in this literature, such as Cassam (2007) and Gomes (2017), seem to hold that natural necessity is *just* causal necessity. On this basis, they endorse the view that the relevant necessary statement is either a priori or natural/causal. In doing so, there is a potential variety of natural necessity that is not in view; namely, the Kripkean (1980) notion of *de re* necessity or necessary a posteriori. This is a natural, albeit non-causal, notion as can be seen in Kripke's classic example of water and H_2O. True, whether this kind of necessity in general really exists is a matter of controversy, and the example from water and H_2O, in particular, is not entirely unproblematic. Still, this kind of natural necessity should at least be considered, and this will be part of our proposal in Section 3.3.

   What about the common suggestion that it might be synthetic a priori, or metaphysically necessary? Since it is in Kant's context, it is indeed natural to think the statement is synthetic a priori. However, it is not clear that this is what Kant intends. Consider his overall project: he asks 'how is synthetic a priori knowledge possible?'. The examples of such knowledge include mathematical knowledge and physics. So for Kant, the possibility of mathematical knowledge (say) requires or presupposes certain psychological machineries. In this case, it is part of the antecedent – the 'Y' of 'the possibility of Y' – that is synthetic a priori. This does not preclude, to be sure, that the entire statement – 'the possibility of Y requires or presupposes X' – is also synthetic a priori, but it is unclear whether this is Kant's actual view, and the very combination of syntheticity and apriority is regarded as problematic anyway, so other things being equal, it should be avoided.

   Stern and Cheng (2023) also suggest that the statement in question is about metaphysical modality. This is indeed an interesting suggestion, and fits our hypothesis as developed in Section 3.3. However, the role the Stern and Cheng (2023) entry assigns to it is not quite accurate. In the entry, metaphysical necessity contrasts with causal or natural necessity. It should be agreed that causal necessity is no metaphysical necessity, but as mentioned, Kripkean *natural* necessity can be metaphysical necessity, as standardly understood in the relevant literature. In fact, there is another option of nomological necessity, which is regarded as a kind of natural necessity, and is different from either metaphysical necessity or causal necessity. Some might even think that nomological possibility is what Kant has in mind. For our purposes, though, we do not consider nomological necessity, that is, the necessity guaranteed by natural laws. In what follows, we will put forward the hypothesis that many transcendental arguments should be understood as involving *de re* necessity in their conditional premises, and this way of understanding those arguments makes them more plausible. In the recent literature, it has been argued that transcendental conditionals are claims about metaphysical possibility, and since they have to be understood via conceivability they are problematic claims (Mizrahi 2017). Stern and Cheng (2023) make the case that this is unfair to transcendental arguments, but the insight that we can keep is that transcendental arguments involve not only modal metaphysics, but also modal *epistemology*.[7]

So what we have here is an understanding of transcendental arguments that is slightly different from what we see in canonical characterisations such as those from SEP. However, this understanding should not be regarded as problematic just because of that. We have provided readers with some reasons to doubt some elements in the canonical picture. To have a fuller understanding, we must dive into the relevant history, as we do in the next section. For now, we should already have a good grasp of how transcendental arguments are standardly understood.

Now, why does Cassam think that transcendental arguments cannot fit the bill for his level 3? Here is a simplified and partial characterisation. Cassam points out that transcendental arguments have been taken to be revelatory, validatory, or explanatory; he then goes on to argue against all of these. Since our notion of possibilitation is *explanatory*, as we will see in Section 3, we will only consider Cassam's case against explanatory transcendental arguments. Although his discussions are complicated, most points are epitomised in the two examples/ analogies he elaborates. One of them is as follows:

---

[7] The basic dialectic is this: Mizrahi (2017) holds that transcendental conditionals *have to be* understood as expressing metaphysical modality, which *has to be* understood with a very strong notion of conceivability, which is problematic. We argue that such a narrow reading of transcendental conditionals is ungrounded.

> Suppose that we are trying to explain what cricket is to someone who doesn't know anything about it ... To know what a game of cricket is, one needs to know something about how it is played and about what winning or losing at cricket consists in but to know these things is not, in any obvious sense, to know the necessary conditions for cricket. Even if we can make sense of the idea that cricket has necessary conditions we can still explain what cricket is without talking in terms of necessary conditions. (Cassam 2007: 81)

This seems correct, but what this shows is that the *kind* of necessary conditions involved in transcendental conditionals is different: If we hold that the possibility of objective cognition requires or presupposes Kantian categories, we not only hold that Kantian categories are necessary (in some sense) for objective cognition; we further hold that Kantian categories *transcendentally explain* the possibility of objective cognition. Or more simply put, Kantian categories *possibilitate* objective cognition. To be sure, the burden is on us: we need to give a positive account about what we mean by 'transcendental explanation' and 'possibilitation', and this is exactly what we will do in Section 3.3. However, it is fair to say at this point that there is *nothing* transcendental in the cricket example; it is no wonder, in that case, that identifying necessary conditions is of no use. Now let's consider the other example from Cassam:

> [I]f someone asks how it is possible to travel from London to Paris in less than three hours, it would be perverse to think that what this question calls for is a specification of the *necessary* conditions for travelling from London to Paris in this time ... starting in London is a necessary condition for travelling from London to Paris but hardly a means of making this journey [which gives the answer to the question]. (Cassam 2007: 52)

Again, Cassam is right about his verdict in this example, but since it is obvious that there is nothing transcendental about such an example, the fact that its necessary condition does not answer the relevant question has no bearing on our transcendental projects. As long as we recognise that the kind of conditions of possibility involved in transcendental conditionals are different from ordinary necessary conditions, we at least open the possibility that such conditions can possibilitate the target. Again, the burden is on us: we need to say how, exactly, possibilitation works. Before providing such a positive account, however, in the next section we will look into the relevant history to see what insights we can distil from those historical discussions. We will then put forward the hypothesis that for transcendental arguments to work, at least in many cases, the key premise (known as 'transcendental conditionals') should be construed as synthetically necessary a posteriori. We will then apply this hypothesis to some prominent putative transcendental arguments in epistemology, and will end with future directions such as naturalising transcendental arguments and how such arguments can mesh with interdisciplinary empirical philosophy. The upshot is that even if the hypothesis put forward is no good, there is still much to learn in thinking through issues concerning transcendental arguments in particular and transcendental epistemology in general.

2 What Are Transcendental Arguments? The History Overviewed

In the previous section, we introduced the area of transcendental epistemology, which is defined by epistemological how-possible questions. We then described the general shape of Quassim Cassam's multi-levels response, and where our primary disagreements are. Later, we discussed the (relatively) standard or canonical conception of contemporary transcendental arguments, and why it might be problematic on many fronts. Finally, we briefly saw Cassam's case against explanatory transcendental arguments, and how we might respond to it. In this section, we will discuss parts of the history of such arguments. As we know, serious studies of the history cannot be conducted with several thousand words, so what will be offered should not be regarded as serious scholarship. However, we do attempt to take the relevant parts of the history seriously: we will go into the history in some detail, and argue that there are aspects of transcendental arguments that can be understood only through careful consideration of the historical development. This remark is of course very abstract; let's go into those materials now to see what we mean.

2.1 Kant and German Idealists

It is often pointed out that transcendental arguments, broadly construed, can be found in the history of Western philosophy before Kant; an often-used example is Aristotle's idea that the possibility of meaningful thought requires or presupposes the principle of non-contradiction, and this is meant to address scepticism concerning such a principle (*Metaphysics* 1005b35–1006a28; see Gottlieb 2019). Another example is Descartes' famous *Cogito*: The possibility of *I think* requires or presupposes *I exist* (Descartes 1641/1993; see Bardon 2006). These can, to be sure, be historical stretches. Here, we do not defend such readings; we just wish to let readers know that Kant might not have been the first one to invoke this kind of inference. However, no one can sensibly deny that transcendental arguments have the most systematic uses in Kant, though the expression 'transcendental argument' might be from P. F. Strawson (1959) and J. L. Austin (1961). Paradigmatic cases include Transcendental Deduction of the Categories, Second Analogy, and Refutation of Idealism.

We will not discuss Second Analogy in what follows, so let's briefly see what a standard interpretation might look like: the possibility of representing objective temporal sequences requires or presupposes that the relevant mental contents involve the concept of causation (Hutton 2019; also see Stern 1999). Now let's turn to Transcendental Deduction (Kant 1787/2007, A84–130; B116–69). Standardly understood, this part of the *First Critique* seems to contain a defence of the following conditional, or at least something close enough: the possibility of experiencing objects given in intuition requires or presupposes that certain a priori concepts can be correctly applicable to experiential objects. The first thing to be noted in discussing this central part is that, as Dieter Henrich (1989) points out, Kant uses the German '*Deduktion*' in the legal sense, and for him, it means *justification* of certain uses of the concepts in question. This is important because we have seen that some might regard transcendental arguments as *deductively valid* in ideal scenarios, but if we stick to Kant's original intention here, something other than logical deduction is in order. In the literature there is a hypothesis that transcendental arguments involve *inference to the best explanation* (Hoffmann 2019; Reynolds 2023). Whether that applies to Kant is controversial, but for now we need to only remember that, at least in Transcendental Deduction, what Kant intends is a certain kind of justification other than logical deduction. It is also often said that what Kant has in mind is *the only possible* explanation, which is excessively strong: how can anyone rule out all the possible alternative explanations? Perhaps, one might think, Kant holds that it is *the only reasonable* explanation. But even this might be too strong, unless it is simply inference to the best explanation.[8]

It is well known that Transcendental Deduction is a response to Hume: roughly, Hume has it that those concepts, notably causation, are not applicable to experiential objects, because no *empirical* justification can be provided for such application (Hume 1739/1978). And given his empiricist principle, if there is no empirical justification, then there is no justification at all. Kant's responses are in effect a rejection of the relevant empiricist principle, and then a proposal about how a *transcendental* justification can be given for those concepts. As discussed in Section 1, it might not be quite right to think that this Transcendental Deduction or justification is a response to scepticism, strictly construed.

---

[8] This issue runs throughout the Element. I will provide a speculative answer at the end, but it must be admitted that it is far from satisfactory. Another difficulty concerns how we should understand inference to the best explanation. Although it is often used in evaluating scientific hypotheses, it also appears in ordinary, common-sense reasoning (Douven 2022). However we understand it, our key notion, *possibilitation*, should look different enough; see Section 3.3 for more detail. I thank a reviewer for pressing me on this.

A huge complication here is that the first edition and the second edition of this part – A-Deduction and B-Deduction respectively – are very different, and there are many readings about each of them and their relations. As indicated, here we do not attempt to provide scholarly valid interpretations of the history; what concerns us is what we can learn about transcendental arguments from the relevant history. One notable point is that whichever interpretation one adopts, there are multiple steps in Transcendental Deduction, and by 'multiple' here we mean 'sometimes more than ten'. For example, according to Pereboom's (2022) 'two-pronged strategy interpretation, Transcendental Deduction involves at least sixteen steps, and then it can finally reach the conclusion. How does this square with the idea that a transcendental argument typically involves only two claims, one of which is a conditional? One natural understanding is that the inferential relation between the antecedent and the consequent is implicit and unobvious, so it takes multiple steps to establish it. In that case, one strategy is to use multiple similar conditionals as bridges. For example, the possibility of A requires B, and given that A is actual, it is possible as well. Then B follows. Now the possibility of B requires C, and given that B is actual, it is possible as well. Then C follows. And so on and so forth.[9] Of course, in practice, things are not so straightforward, but it is not unreasonable to expect that many if not all steps can be paraphrased like that. Whether that fits Kant's intention, to be sure, is a difficult historical question that we do not seek to answer.

Refutation of Idealism is similar in that it involves multiple steps, but its status as a transcendental argument is different. Stern and Cheng (2023) have it that this part of the *First Critique* is perhaps *the* paradigm of transcendental arguments: 'Perhaps because of its brevity and relative clarity, but also perhaps because of the hope it can be made "self-standing" and independent of the (to some) disreputable machinery of transcendental idealism, it is the Refutation that has become the paradigm to many of a transcendental argument.' By contrast, David Bell (1999) holds that the Refutation is actually the 'wrong paradigm' precisely because it can be detached from the transcendental inquiry embedded in the German idealist tradition. Which verdict is correct? Here, we adopt a pluralist approach: if we conceive of transcendental arguments as *a distinctive method within Kant's philosophical outlook*, then we should perhaps side with Bell; but if we conceive transcendental arguments as *a distinctive inferential form distilled from Kant's philosophy*, then we should perhaps side with Stern and Cheng. We will largely follow the latter route, with

---

[9] One might wonder how we can avoid deductive reasoning here. More generally, if we still want any notion of necessary conditions, it might be really difficult to avoid deductive reasoning.

full acknowledgement that Bell has a point about the internal connection between transcendental arguments and overarching transcendental inquiry.[10]

Without going into the details of these arguments, we can learn two crucial distinctions from the contrast between Transcendental Deduction and Refutation of Idealism. One of them is between *progressive* and *regressive* transcendental arguments. According to Franks (1999: 116):

> Progressive: Arguments that proceed from ground to grounded.
>
> Regressive: Arguments that regress from grounded to ground. (See also Ameriks 2003.)

Given this distinction, we can understand Transcendental Deduction as *regressive*, and Refutation of Idealism as *progressive*. What does that mean? Take an even simpler toy version of Transcendental Deduction: the possibility of objective cognition requires categories. In this case, the grounded is objective cognition (antecedent). By what? By the categories. Now take a toy version of Refutation of Idealism: the possibility of temporal experience requires awareness of the external world. In this case, the grounded is awareness of the external world (consequent). By what? By temporal experience. This is one reason why formal logic cannot capture the nature of transcendental arguments: while progressive and regressive arguments have the opposite emphases, formal logic can only capture the relation between sufficient and necessary conditions (cf. Harrison 1982; see also Tse 2020 for the other premise, the so-called self-knowledge premise). Note that this distinction also plays an important role in Cassam's (2007: ch. 2) discussion, but the labels he invokes are 'regressive' and 'anti-sceptical', which is not exactly apt, because it implies that progressive arguments have to be anti-sceptical. They might be co-extensive in most cases, because a common reason why the consequent needs to be gro.unded is that it is challenged by sceptics, but as we have argued, scepticism has a specific meaning in philosophy and being too liberal about this term can be problematic. Therefore I recommend that we keep the distinction between progressive and regressive transcendental arguments.

The other crucial distinction is between *world-directed* and *self-directed* transcendental arguments:

> World-directed: Arguments that tell us something about the nature of the world.[11]
>
> Self-directed: Arguments that tell us something about the cognitive faculties of the thinking or knowing self. (Cassam 1999: 85)

---

[10] Bell's insistence on this point was confirmed in recent personal communications.
[11] This is virtually the same as 'truth-directed' in Peacocke (1989).

This needs qualifications, to be sure: As we should readily acknowledge, all thinking or knowing selves are also *in the world*, unless we have very special ontologies; so when we say 'the nature of the world' in this context, we mean 'the nature of the world *other than the subject in question*'. Now given this distinction, we can understand Transcendental Deduction as *self-directed*, and Refutation of Idealism as *world-directed*. What does that mean? Again if we understand Transcendental Deduction in this simplified way – the possibility of objective cognition requires categories – then since categories are our cognitive faculties, this argument is self-directed. As for Refutation of Idealism, if we understand it in this simplified way – the possibility of temporal experience requires awareness of the external world – then since awareness of the external world involves the external world itself, this argument is world-directed.[12] Just as with the previous distinction between the progressive and the regressive, this distinction between the world-directed and the self-directed also cannot be captured by formal logic, for such a distinction is about the actual contents of the arguments. This distinction will resurface soon in Section 3 when we discuss analytical revivals in the twentieth century.

When it comes to world-directed transcendental arguments, one needs to be wary of Barry Stroud's (1968) simple and powerful objection that the move from the psychological to the non-psychological by this kind of ambitious transcendental argument in unwarranted. On this occasion, I make the conservative assumption that, if possible, transcendental arguments should stay self-directed and moderate. I shall stay neutral about whether one can come up with good responses to Stroud's objection, and will not dwell on this point. The reason is that there have been so many pieces on transcendental arguments that focus on Stroud's position, notably the SEP entry, the IEP entry, and various papers in Stern (1999). However, these do not touch on some important aspects of transcendental arguments, such as the distinction between the progressive and the regressive we have introduced here. Therefore, for the sake of good divisions of labour, in this Element we will not discuss the Stroud dialectics in detail. To be sure, this is not to downplay the importance of ambitious, world-directed transcendental arguments: both Descartes' *Cogito* argument and Kant's Refutation of Idealism are potential important examples. Given space limitations, I defer such discussions to the previous literature (e.g., Foote 1994, for the transcendental interpretation of Descartes), though I will say a bit more about Stroud in Section 2.3.

---

[12] A controversy here is that if the conclusion includes 'awareness of the external world', it might still be self-directed because awareness is a mental episode. This heavily relies on how we construe the conclusion of Kant's Refutation of Idealism.

Following Kant's substantive reliance on transcendental arguments, this strategy was variously developed by German idealists such as Reinhold, Fichte, Schelling, and Hegel; German empiricists such as Schulze; rationalist sceptics such as Maimon; psychologism proposed by Niethammer. We cannot cover them all, and we cannot offer scholarly discussions, but since contemporary discussions of transcendental arguments tend to jump from Kant to the twentieth century, some insights from the eighteenth and nineteenth centuries can be missed if one does not discuss them at all. According to Paul Franks, Reinhold attempts 'to systemize Kant's philosophy by transforming it into a single transcendental argument' which generates subsequent discussions of Schulze and Fichte (Franks 1999: 112; for an objection to this reading, see Rosen 1999). Reinhold's *Elementarphilosophie* (1789) is a direct development of Kant's methods and systems; more specifically, he believes that the forms of intuition, the categories, the moral laws, and all the important Kantian notions can be derived from a further groundwork and, ultimately, an absolute first principle. To further understand what this amounts to, we need to introduce yet another distinction between versions of transcendental arguments; here are Franks' formulations:

> Analytic: The conditions are reached by conceptual analysis and the negation of the resulting conditional is a contradiction.

> Synthetic: They are alternatives, or supplements, to conceptual analysis and establish conditions that are the negations, not of contradictions, but of putative thoughts that are necessarily ruled out in some other way. (Franks 1999: 117–18)

It is important to note that the analytic/synthetic terminologies are terms of art that are especially complicated in modern philosophy. For example, the characterisations here are different from the ones in Kant's (1783/1994) *Prolegomena*. For our purposes, we will stick to the descriptions just given. It is a difficult interpretative question as to whether Kant's transcendental arguments, specifically the conditionals, are analytic or synthetic. As we have discussed, it is too hasty to assume that since synthetic a priori judgements play crucial roles in Kant's philosophy, transcendental conditionals must be such judgements (see also Franks 1999: 119). What we should say is that part of the antecedent, for example, mathematical propositions, are synthetic a priori. A further complication is that even if the conditional in question is analytic, the entire argument can still be synthetic, as other premises might be synthetic. This is a general point that is applicable to all transcendental arguments. Here, of course, we are assuming that such a distinction can still survive after Quine's (1953) severe attack. It is worth pointing out that although most philosophers nowadays reject Quine's version of physicalism, scientism, behaviouralism, and so on, they still accept his attacks on analyticity. However, those attacks largely hinge on the above 'isms', so it is unclear whether the contemporary rejection of analyticity based on Quinean reasons is justified.[13]

Now, why do we need to introduce this distinction at this point? The reason is that, at least according to Franks' interpretation, Reinhold's transcendental arguments are *analytic regressive*, while Fichte's are *synthetic progressive*. This is a big division within German idealism, which has consequences for the subsequent history. Later, when we discuss transcendental arguments from phenomenologists and analytic philosophers (Sections 2.2 and 2.3), it is crucial to get clear what versions they have in mind. As we shall see, in most cases it is often not so clear. A general point from Franks' (1999) paper is that if Fichte and Hegel can be said to invoke transcendental arguments at all, theirs are more like synthetic-progressive ones, which are different from contemporary analytic-regressive ones. This point, to be sure, is controversial and obviously not universally agreed (Taylor 1975; Neuhouser 1990).

With these sketchy discussions of Kant and the German idealists, we have introduced three crucial distinctions: The progressive and the regressive; the world-directed (ambitious) and the self-directed (moderate); and the analytic and the synthetic. These are conceptual tools we can rely on in further inquiries. Now we will turn to some transcendental arguments in the phenomenological tradition. Like the current section, our discussions in the next subsection will not be anything like historical scholarship. The primary aim of going through these histories, albeit sketchily, is to have some basic ideas about what has been done, and what conceptual resources we can use. Now let's turn to some examples of transcendental arguments in phenomenology.

2.2 Phenomenologists

Very roughly, the phenomenological tradition was founded by Edmund Husserl, who was influenced by Franz Brentano. It is not hard to see why transcendental arguments might be important elements in this tradition, given that many phases of Husserl's philosophy are *transcendental* phenomenology, and that later practitioners such as Heidegger, Sartre, and Merleau-Ponty all have some transcendental elements in their versions of phenomenology. This, however, is very impressionistic, so concrete examples are in order. This subsection is divided into two parts. The first half will provide a general picture of the

---

[13] I vaguely remember that I heard this observation from Nathan Salmón in a session on Kripke at the Pacific Division American Philosophical Assocation meeting 2023, but I cannot be sure about this.

phenomenological tradition and explain in what sense phenomenologists are engaging in *transcendental epistemology*. The second half will look into specific examples of transcendental arguments that can be found in the phenomenologists, and see what we can learn from those arguments.

What is phenomenology? It is impractical to expect a succinct answer to this question in the present context. However, if we can begin with a slogan, one option is this: *from the manifest to the essential*; that is, we first reflect on our own conscious experiences' manifest properties and somehow move to those experiences' essential properties (Ward 2021). 'Essence' here is supposed to be contrasted with 'facts', which are studied by empirical sciences. *Transcendental epistemology*, in this context, is the pursuit of the essential properties of one's own conscious experiences by asking epistemological how-possible questions. More specifically, we are looking for formal and invariant properties of experiences, that is, features they must have or must lack (Gomes 2017). In this sense, Kant and even Hume might be proto-phenomenologists. Of course, they do not, strictly speaking, qualify as phenomenologists – to qualify, varieties of *phenomenological reductions* identified by Husserl need to be conducted – but for our purposes, we can stick to the slogan cited, with more elaborations to follow.

Consider Kant's Second Analogy of Experience in the *First Critique*: again roughly, the possibility of experiencing something happening requires or presupposes the application of causal concepts (Kant 1787/2007: A195/B240). This fits the slogan because one knows one is experiencing something happening by reflecting on those experiences (the manifest), and somehow moves to the conclusion that the application of causal concepts is necessary for that (the essential). In this sense, Kant is engaging transcendental phenomenology here, though without explicitly invoking any phenomenological reduction: in this sense, transcendental phenomenology 'reflects on the condition of possibility that must be fulfilled in order for experience to manifest itself to us in the way it does' (Ward 2021: 238). Thus, Kant goes beyond Hume's project of identifying a 'mere quirk of human psychology' (Ward 2021: 236).

Since we should all agree that Kant does not engage in phenomenology proper, let's see how the founder of that tradition conceives of it. Very generally, Husserl understands phenomenology as a branch of philosophy that seeks to uncover the essential a priori structures governing psychological episodes. In this respect, Husserl regards himself as conducting a Kantian transcendental project that purports to investigate how the manifolds of conscious experiences are regulated by the relevant essential structural properties of consciousness. One crucial point where Husserl goes beyond Kant is *eidetic variation*, an activity that discovers essence (*eidos*) via imaginatively varying aspects of conscious experiences to see what has to remain constant to ensure the identity of such experiences (Husserl 1913/2012). This is a surprising precursor of contemporary rationalist modal epistemology in the Anglo-Saxon tradition: two major sub-groups of this approach are the *conceivability* view (Yablo 1993; Chalmers 2002) and the *essentialist* view (Lowe 2008, 2012). Although there have been heated family quarrels within modal rationalism between these two views, we see how they can be combined in Husserl's picture. Through conceivability and inconceivability, the essence of conscious experiences can be uncovered. This, however, means that objections to modal rationalism might plague Husserlian eidetic variation. Note that Kant's transcendental arguments have also been interpreted as conceivability arguments (Mizrahi 2017), as mentioned in Section 1, but there are two caveats: first, whether such an interpretation is historically correct is controversial, and second, even if we view both Kant's and Husserl's projects as variants of the conceivability approach, there is still one huge divergence between them. While Kant, perhaps more like contemporary analytic metaphysicians, regards this process as *discursive*, Husserl regards it as *intuitive*. This might be yet another distinction for transcendental arguments. To enter this subtle difference will take us too far, so we shall stay in our mainline.

Even if we tentatively agree that the all-too-brief characterisation of Husserl's phenomenological framework given here is more or less intelligible, it is hasty to think that such a framework is shared by later famous phenomenologists. As many would agree, each phenomenologist has her/his distinctive take on what phenomenology is or should be (e.g., Spiegelberg 1981). Since this is not the place to provide an introduction to the phenomenological tradition, we shall again stick to simplifications. While the later Husserl emphasises the importance of *the body*, Heidegger focusses more on our relations to *the meaningful world*, and Merleau-Ponty synthesises all these and further considers *historical and cultural elements* in the transcendental structuring of the human mind. Without diverging into these different frameworks, we will move to the second half of this subsection, that is, to specific examples of potential transcendental arguments in the phenomenological tradition.

The examples we will briefly survey are primarily about other minds and intersubjectivity. There have been many formulations of philosophical puzzles about other minds; here is one from Husserl: 'how can my ego, within his peculiar ownness, constitute under the name "experience of something other," precisely something *other*' (Husserl 1931/1977: 94, original italics). From this, we can see that this formulation does not concern the *existence* of other minds, but our *experience of* or awareness of other minds. Two comments are in order. First, this clearly fits the general phenomenological outlook, that is, focussing on conscious experiences themselves; or, more specifically, on objects (including other minds) as presented in our experiences. Second, this makes the aims of transcendental arguments more reasonable and moderate in that if the conclusion is something about our *experiences of* other minds, this would require only *self-directed* transcendental arguments, which are less ambitious than world-directed or truth-directed ones.

Now, just as Kant never uses the German term corresponding to 'transcendental arguments', Husserl speaks of 'transcendental reflection' instead. This might have a further implication in the Husserlian context, in that his phenomenological project is *descriptive*, rather than *argumentative*. It has been pointed out, however, that this contrast might be exaggerated in this context (Reynolds 2023): although both Brentano and Husserl emphasise the *descriptive* nature of their projects, it is not as if they do not embed *arguments* in those texts. So does Husserl invoke anything like transcendental arguments? Here is one potential place to look, as described by Russell and Reynolds (2011: 302, original italics):

> According to Husserl's reflections, various modes of experience exhibit a hierarchical structure; conscious acts are more or less 'basic' to the extent that they presuppose other conscious acts. For example, the *judgement* that a retaining wall is collapsing is less basic than a mere *perception* of the wall as a retaining wall, since the consciousness of the state of affairs asserted in the judgement is 'founded' upon the consciousness of the perceptual object. There is, then, a hierarchy, or order of presupposition, among conscious acts due to the 'logic' of experience itself.

The line of thought is that the founding relations are uncovered via transcendental reflections, and such presuppositions can be seen as transcendental conditions of possibility.

Now let's look into a specific example. In later works, Husserl seems to hold that the possibility of experiencing transcendence, objectivity, reality, and so on, requires or presupposes a 'community of egos' (Husserl 1931/1977: 107). Now, recall that here we only require *experiences* of a community of egos, so it might seem that such a requirement is easy to meet. However, even if it is weaker than the existence of other minds, it is questionable whether experiences of a *community* of egos is required. The antecedent is about objective experiences: Couldn't we easily imagine that someone can perceive something as mind-independent, that is, 'object permanence' in the sense defined by developmental psychology (Bremner 1994), but without experiencing anyone else? What about someone who luckily survives for a short while without any support from a caregiver? To make things more vivid, consider other animals: can't a cat perceive rats as mind-independent, even if the cat has not experienced 'a community of egos'? This kind of challenge affects other similar arguments too, such as Davidson's (1987, 1991) anti-sceptical argument concerning other minds based on the 'triangulation' thought experiment. Now, whether Husserl and his followers can defend the transcendental conditional cited depends partly on what Husserl says in that context: He not only proposes such a connection between the possibility of objective experiences and experiences of other minds, but also writes much about why such connection holds. For our purposes, though, we will not evaluate his overall reasonings.

Again, although Husserl was the founder of the phenomenological tradition, there have been so many important phenomenologists after him, and some of them have proposed something like transcendental arguments. Examples include Heidegger's (1927/2008) idea that the possibility of human existence requires or presupposes the structure of 'Being-with' and Sartre's (1943/2021) idea that the possibility of shame requires or presupposes experiencing oneself being caught by others. It is likely that given their different attitudes toward Kant's project, they might not be happy with these simplifications, but at least by presenting their ideas like this we have a rough idea about how transcendental arguments might work in the phenomenological tradition.

There is one crucial potential divergence between the Kantians and the phenomenologists that is worth highlighting. While in Kant and many others, conditions of *possibility* are the key part of transcendental arguments, for Merleau-Ponty, and perhaps Deleuze, what should be central are conditions of *actuality* (Inkpin 2016). One interpretation is that they have transformed transcendental arguments into a different mode. Another, and preferred, interpretation is that they are already too different from the Kantian spirit, so perhaps should not be classified as any kind of transcendental argument. Relatedly, phenomenology has generated very rich contemporary continental philosophy, including thoughts from Foucault, Habermas, and Apel. What about their sociopolitical critiques? Should they be considered as branches of transcendental epistemology? I let readers decide for themselves.[14]

2.3 Analytical Revivals

As we know, transcendental arguments had their renaissance in the Anglo-Saxon tradition in the second half of the twentieth century. However, it is not as if earlier analytic philosophers made no contribution to this movement: since transcendental arguments are characteristically first person given that they have very uncontroversial starting points; first-person reflections on one's own experiences have a crucial role to play. As Anil Gomes (2017: 138) points out, Moore (1925), Cook Wilson (1926), Price (1932), and Prichard (1938) all

---

[14] I thank a reviewer for pointing me in these directions.

emphasise the idea that 'the first-person perspective can reveal truths about the nature of perceptual experience'. However, we will focus on the second half of the twentieth century, as emphasising the first-person method is not, by itself, sufficient for transcendental argumentations.

A common starting point in this regard is P. F. Strawson's argumentative strategy, exemplified in his *Individuals* (1959), *The Bounds of Sense* (1966), and various other writings. One prominent example is the 'objectivity argument' (Strawson 1966), which is a critical commentary on Kant's *Critique of Pure Reason*. The argument seeks to show that '[u]nity of diverse experiences in a single consciousness requires experience of objects' (Strawson 1966: 203). More specifically, the argument begins with the idea that being self-conscious amounts to the capacity for ascribing diverse experiences to oneself, while being conscious of the unity of that to which they are ascribed. In order to be able to conceive of experiences as one's own, one must be able to conceive of them as experiences. This further requires that one can grasp the distinction between 'this is how things are experienced as being' (appearance) and 'this is how things are' (reality). Now, only experiences of objects that are mind-independent, that is, objective, could provide room for this distinction between appearance and reality. Thus, there are objects that exist in a mind-independent way. This is what Strawson means by 'objectivity in the weighty sense' (see Strawson 1966: roughly 97–112).

Why is this a transcendental argument? One obvious observation is that it involves transitions such as 'requires' and 'must be able to', and these are usual terms invoked in transcendental conditionals. But this is not enough by itself. Another crucial point is whether the starting point of the argument begin with the *possibility* of certain specific phenomena. Strawson's wording here does not have that explicitly, so this complicates the matter. Note that people like Davidson also do not begin with 'the possibility of . . .'; rather, Davidson (1989) begins with 'the existence of thoughts'. Does this mean that the entire construction beginning with 'the possibility of . . .' is wrongheaded? This is not so. What these philosophers have in mind, or at least some of them, is what we normally call 'the condition of possibility' (e.g., Zahavi 2007, on the Heidelberg School). For example, the claim might be that human thoughts exist, and one condition of their possibility is the awareness of another creature with thoughts. The crucial point here is thus how to understand 'the condition of possibility'. In the literature, it is normally understood as a version of necessary conditions. However, not all necessary conditions are supposed to be conditions of possibility, otherwise transcendental arguments would not be distinctive at all; recall our discussion of Cassam's examples from cricket and travelling from London to Paris in Section 1.3. To understand what this kind of condition amounts to is the major aim of this Element, especially Section 3.

Another prominent example from Strawson is his 'no-space world' thought experiment (Strawson 1959), which is notoriously difficult to interpret. Here, the aim is not to provide a detailed and authoritative reconstruction of the arguments in this work. We will look into some aspects of them, with the emphasis on their relation to modal epistemology and metaphysics. It is particularly apt to discuss this relation here because thought experiments and metaphysical possibility often go hand in hand. Now, *Individuals* (Strawson 1959) belongs to what Strawson calls 'descriptive metaphysics'. By the end of the first chapter, he reaches the first major conclusion that material bodies are basic to particular-identification in our *actual* conceptual scheme. This is a controversial claim that we will not examine here. In the second chapter, Strawson proceeds to ask whether there could be an *alternative* conceptual scheme that still involves objective and identifiable particulars, but in which material bodies are non-basic. Strawson's answer seems to be that there *could* be such a scheme, and this is where the no-space world or sound-only world comes in. After this point, the exact interpretation of Strawson's view is contested: Gareth Evans (1980) interprets Strawson as holding that objectivity requires spatiality, while Paul Snowdon (2019) holds the opposite view. Regardless of which side we are on, we can understand the claim here in transcendental terms:

The possibility of objective reference requires or presupposes spatiality.

While Evans believes Strawson affirms this statement, Snowdon does not. For our purposes, let's focus on the thesis itself. How should we proceed in deciding whether it is plausible? Following our previous discussion, the modal rationalist approach would suggest that we examine the following statement:

It is *inconceivable* that there is objective reference without spatiality.

This is not supposed to be a paraphrase, which would be too strong; it is just one's *epistemic* way of figuring out how plausible the original statement is. Now let's look into the thought experiment itself. Strawson begins with the traditional classification of the five outer senses. The chemical senses – olfaction and gustation – are set aside quickly, as losing them would not change people's world view, or so it seems to Strawson. Touch with kinaesthesia would presumably bring in spatiality, so it should be set aside too in this context. Sight is obviously spatial, so it is out of the question. This leaves us with audition and sounds: if in the no-space world there are sounds, and a certain creature possesses the relevant capacities for hearing sounds, would that creature be able to refer to targets objectively? Is it conceivable or inconceivable that there is *objective reference without spatiality*?

Now, a natural objection is that sounds are *obviously spatial*: we can hear sounds coming from different directions, and from different distances. Strawson here draws a distinction between *intrinsic* and *derivative* spatiality: he holds that while vision is intrinsically spatial, touch and audition are not. This is why he thinks touch needs to be coupled with kinaesthesia to be spatial. This claim has been challenged empirically (Cheng 2019), but at this point we will focus on sounds and audition. Strawson argues that auditory properties are all non-spatial *in themselves*; they gain their spatiality via cross-modal interactions with other sense modalities.

Now one might still feel unconvinced. For the sake of our explorations, let's grant Strawson this point and proceed. Assuming that sounds are not intrinsically spatial, then what? If in the no-space world there are sounds only, can the creature develop the capacities for objective reference without spatiality? On this view of sounds, they are *purely temporal individuals*. So we are, in effect, asking: can a universe with purely temporal individuals accommodate objective reference? This is why in chapter 2, Strawson (1959) considers *series* of sounds, and a 'master-sound' that serves as a temporal coordinate or framework to anchor other sounds. After a rich, though long-winded, discussion of this thought experiment, Strawson admits that the situation is too abstract and unclear, so in chapter 3 he comes back to more concrete discussions on persons (Strawson 1959). This at least partially explains why Evans and Snowdon ended up with opposing interpretations of Strawson's view. In order to implement our understanding of transcendental conditionals, let's follow Evans' suggestion. To anticipate, the picture that will be developed in the next section suggests that we should hold that spatiality is *part of the essence* of objective reference: it is essential to objectively referring to anything that a certain kind of spatiality is in place. But does this mean that spatiality in any sense can *explain* objective reference? Again, we will need to wait until Section 3 to see the relation between imagination and *possibilitation* as the relevant kind of transcendental explanation.

One notable point about Strawson's project, which can be labelled 'Oxford Kantianism' (Cheng 2021), is that he conducts these arguments without appealing to transcendental idealism, or the 'doctrines of transcendental psychology' (Strawson 1966: 97; cf. Kitcher 1993). For Strawson and some of his followers, this is a merit of the approach, as they deem transcendental idealism as doomed to fail. However, as Stroud (1968) and others have observed, whether world-directed transcendental arguments can do without such a doctrine is questionable; it is as if the conditional seeks to move from the psychological to the non-psychological, and it is unclear whether the inference would work if the consequent is entirely mind-independent. To be sure, transcendental idealism is not the only link that can bridge the antecedent and the consequent: what is needed is a doctrine that collapses the distinction between appearance and reality. After all, the main difficulty of world-directed transcendental arguments is the leap from the psychological to the non-psychological, so if in certain domains the psychological is *everything* that is the case, then the inference might be easier to make.

A common example is *verificationism*, the idea that the ontology of meaning is determined by how the meaning-bearers are verified (Rorty 1971). Why is it supposed to be helpful? If the ontology of meaning is not independent of how one verifies the meaning-bearers, then the gap from the psychological to the non-psychological is bridged: given verificationism of some sort, the non-psychological is determined by the psychological (Bennett 1979; Brueckner 1984). This move, however, obviously incurs new problems. Although every idea in philosophy is in principle defensible to some extent, verificationism is so out of fashion and problematic that if transcendental arguments need to be combined with it for it to work, then so much the worse for such arguments. Moreover, it might make transcendental arguments redundant in that if one already subscribes to verificationism, the desired conclusion can be reached anyway. This combination can be found in Wittgenstein's notion of 'criteria' in relation to the problem of other minds, so there is some historical interest in such a theoretical move. In addition to verificationism, *phenomenalism* is another option (Brueckner 1984), but it doesn't make things any better. Although the dialectic can get very complicated (Stroud 1968, 1999, 2011; see also Cassam 1987), the general moral is that to avoid combining transcendental arguments with (transcendental) idealism, verificationism, or phenomenalism, they should not be world-directed (ambitious), but should be self-directed (modest). In this regard, Transcendental Deduction is indeed a better paradigm than the Refutation of Idealism, one might think.[15]

The analytical revivals are of course not confined to Strawson's arguments. Other well-known cases include Shoemaker (1963) on self-knowledge, Putnam (1981) on brain-in-a-vat, Kripke (1982) on Wittgenstein and rule-following, Davidson (1987, 1991) on triangulation and varieties of knowledge, O'Shaughnessy (1980, 1989; see also Bermúdez 1995; Stern and Cheng

---

[15] There might be another potential problem if we go into theories of consciousness here. For example, if one holds *illusionism*, the idea that conscious experiences do not really have phenomenal properties (Dennett 1991; Frankish 2016), one might thereby believe that we cannot infer anything from conscious experiences. Although we cannot address this worry entirely here, we hold the conservative view that even if conscious experiences are all illusory in the relevant sense, we can still draw certain conclusions from them. For example, the possibility of my allegedly illusory experiences requires that I have spatio-temporal forms of intuitions. Illusionism will, to be sure, make even more trouble for world-directed arguments. I thank a reviewer for urging me to be clear about this.

2023) on intentional actions and bodily awareness, and Korsgaard (1996, 1998) on valuing oneself, to name just a few. This makes the project of understanding transcendental arguments even more pressing: If such arguments are doomed to fail, and if the examples cited are really instances of such arguments, then they are all in big trouble. There would be no need to wrestle with all the intricate details of those discussions, as the argumentative strategy they invoke was flawed. In Section 3, we will discuss one way that might make transcendental arguments defensible: The transcendental conditionals should be synthetic; they should embody Kripkean (1980) *de re* necessity claims; and a specific philosophical explanation – possibilitation – should be in place to make transcendental arguments distinctive.

3 What Should Transcendental Arguments Be? A Hypothesis Proposed

We have seen that what *are*, or what *were*, transcendental arguments historically. To emphasise again, the historical overview we have offered is very sketchy, and it is hard to claim historical scholarship in this kind of context. Still, we have some rough ideas about how philosophers have conceived of such arguments, and what kinds of major objections have been raised. We are now in a better position to discuss how such arguments *should* be: how they should be conceived so that they can be philosophically effective arguments. In what follows, we will first propose that good transcendental conditionals should perhaps be synthetic, rather than analytic. Then we will move to our bold hypothesis that maybe such conditionals should be a certain kind of *de re* necessity statements. And finally, we will elaborate the idea that the kind of philosophical explanations offered by transcendental arguments are distinctive: they are neither *scientific empirical* explanations nor *metaphysical grounding* explanations. Rather, they are *metaphysical cum transcendental* explanations. This serves as our response to Cassam's challenge that was identified in Section 1.

3.1 Syntheticity

The terminological pair 'analytic' and 'synthetic' has generated many problems in philosophy. To begin with, Kant uses these terms in more than one way. It is safe to say that what we mean here is *not* what Kant means in *Prolegomena* (Kant 1783/1994). To prevent complications, we will go with this rough-and-ready understanding:

Analyticity: The truth value of the statement in question can be fully determined by the meanings of the terms in that statement. [True in virtue of meaning.]

In doing so, we may bypass the convoluted evolution of such a notion, but let's still have a look of the standard account of it, since such an account helps us think through issues in this section. Something like analyticity can at least be traced back to Hume, specifically his distinction between 'relations of ideas' and 'matters of fact'; this is the so-called Hume's fork. The former is often seen as a precursor of analyticity. One interesting point is that Hume combines his fork with another distinction between *conceivability* and inconceivability: For him, propositions about relations of ideas are independent of what exists in reality, and the negation of this kind of proposition is *inconceivable* and therefore *contradictory* and *impossible*. By contrast, propositions about matters of fact are about what exists in reality, so the truths of such propositions need to be determined with the help of sensory experiences. The negation of this kind of proposition is *conceivable* or *intelligible* and therefore *non-contradictory* and *possible*.

Here we can clearly see that, in Hume, several issues are not sufficiently distinguished: from a contemporary point of view, the analytic/synthetic distinction is *semantic* (see the rough-and-ready understanding discussed), while whether something is justified or known only via sensory experiences is *epistemological*, and whether something is conceivable, intelligible, possible, and so on, is *metaphysical*. The distinction between the three domains became sharp after Kripke (1980), and there will be more on this in the next subsection. For now, what we need to keep in mind is that when we ask whether transcendental conditionals are analytic or synthetic, we are focussing on semantic issues. That being said, epistemological and metaphysical issues are highly related. For example, there are issues concerning whether we should invoke *metaphysical necessity* to understand transcendental conditionals, and issues concerning how notions such as conceivability, essence, and so on, can help us determine the truth values of such conditionals (Stern and Cheng, 2023). These will be covered in the following subsection. For now, let's stick to the semantic issues.

Although Kant accepts many ideas from Hume, he famously challenges the view that a priori judgements *have to be* analytic. For Kant, the sources of a priori knowledge are a priori intuitions, a priori concepts, and some knowledge about rules. He believes that judgements such as 'all objects are extended' are analytic a priori, while '5 + 7 = 12' and certain judgements in Euclidean geometry are synthetic a priori. Now, Kant's picture here is highly controversial: his definition of analyticity involving a certain notion of 'containment', his examples of synthetic judgements, his insistence on the existence of synthetic a priori judgements, and so on, have all been disputed for hundreds of years. For our purposes, though, we bracket all these challenges. What we should bear in mind is that even if we accept everything Kant's says in this regard, it is still hasty, or even wrong, to think that Kant holds that transcendental conditionals are, or should be, synthetic a priori, as we have indicated. As this point is so very important, we shall emphasise it again. Consider this toy example:

The possibility of geometry requires or presupposes a priori intuitions.

For Kant, (Euclidean) geometry's validity as a subject matter is *actual*; what concerns him is the *foundation* of this validity. He holds that certain propositions in geometry are synthetic a priori, and the question is about *how it is possible* to entertain such judgements. That is to say, what is synthetic a priori are propositions in geometry, not the transcendental conditional in question. To be sure, what's just been said does not preclude the conditional from also being synthetic a priori, but there is no clear evidence for the idea that Kant holds such a view, and it is unclear why we should regard those conditionals as synthetic a priori either.

We will come back to Kant frequently, for obvious reasons. The analytic/synthetic distinction in the relevant sense continued to evolve in Western philosophy; important thinkers such as Bolzano, Frege, Russell, Carnap, and so on, all play critical roles in the development of this distinction. Famously, Quine (1953) challenges the distinction by casting doubts on notions of analyticity, apriority, necessity, synonymity, and so forth. If he is right, all assertions or propositions are synthetic, if that notion makes sense at all. That is, their truth values cannot be determined by semantic analysis; there is no such thing as 'true in virtue of meaning'. In that case, transcendental conditionals should all be synthetic. Now, here our proposal is less radical: the idea is that for *some* transcendental conditionals to work, they should be understood as synthetic propositions. This leaves open the possibility that some transcendental conditionals are or should be understood as analytic. Again, Quinean reasons for rejecting analyticity might be themselves problematic.

Now why should some of those conditionals be understood as synthetic? Consider this following toy example:

The possibility of objective cognition requires or presupposes Kantian categories.

To understand such a conditional as analytic is to think that if it is true, it is true in virtue of meanings involved in the statement alone. To do this, one needs to begin with clear definitions of the concepts involved, including objectivity, cognition, categories, possibility, and so forth. And one needs to make the case that sheerly by analysing those concepts, the truth of the conditional can be established. While this is indeed a possible view, here we propose the hypothesis that even though it is sensible to begin with clear definitions of those concepts, it is more plausible to think that conceptual analysis by itself is *not* enough to establish the truth of such a conditional. Here is why. On the one hand, to understand what objective cognition consists in, one needs to look into the developmental psychology and animal cognition literatures, and anchor the meaning of it to *empirical* considerations. On the other hand, to understand what categories in the relevant sense consist in, one needs to look into Kant's reason for appropriating the classic judgement table, and whether it is reasonable to do so (see e.g., Snowdon 2017, for questioning why the concept of the first person is not included). Now, to determine whether the conditional is analytic or synthetic, we need to consider the *semantic* relation between these two notions. Is it reasonable to expect that after anchoring the meaning of 'objective cognition' to the developmental psychology and animal cognition literatures, we can then analyse it and discover that categories in the Kantian sense are its conditions of possibility? Although there seems to be no knock-down argument against the analytic reading, it seems more natural to think that just by analysing such an empirical concept (objective cognition), Kantian categories *cannot* be determined as the conditions of possibility of that concept. After all, such a conditional, true or false, looks radically different from mathematical and logical statements, and it is also quite dissimilar to paradigm examples of analyticity such as 'all bachelors are unmarried men': it is simply *not* the kind of thing one can realise by looking into any dictionary. Therefore, we tentatively conclude that, at least for some transcendental conditionals, the synthetic understanding is more apt as a model.

This argument might look weak to some readers. Other subsidiary reasons will be provided in Section 3.2: the idea that such conditionals are synthetic chimes well with the idea that they are necessary a posteriori, which will be explained in the next subsection. Also, in Section 4 we will look into several examples in the extant literature, and it will be suggested that to understand those conditionals as analytic risks trivialising the philosophical significance in question.

3.2 *De Re* Necessity

No matter if you have been persuaded by the syntheticity reading, the consensus is that it is a *semantic* issue, which should be distinguished from the *epistemic* issue (a priori or not) and from the *metaphysical* issue (necessary or not). Let's begin with the former. There seems to be an overwhelming consensus that transcendental conditionals are, or even have to be, a priori. It is unclear why this is assumed without argument, but one speculation is that it might be thought that such statements are outcomes of philosophical reflections, so should be a priori. If one thinks those conditionals are analytic, then one risks trivialising the enterprise. If one instead thinks those conditionals are synthetic, one commits to the view that the transcendental conditionals in question are synthetic a priori. As argued in Section 2.1, it is unclear that Kant regards transcendental conditionals as synthetic a priori. Also, the very idea of synthetic a priori might be difficult to defend. One way out is to regard (some) transcendental conditionals as a posteriori. But how? Let's return to the toy example employed in the previous subsection. For the conditional to be justified a priori, after learning the notion of 'objective cognition' and the notion of 'categories', and so on, one can simply be justified in accepting the conditional purely by rational reflection. But can one? Notice that the conditional in question looks like an *empirical* claim: we need to determine first which kinds of creatures enjoy objective cognition, and which of them have the capacity for using (some of) the Kantian categories. After that, one needs to figure out the relation between the two. There might be empirical counterexamples: perhaps some actual creatures can enjoy objective cognition without the relevant capacity for Kantian categories. This is the kind of matter that requires empirical investigation. So, on the face of it, at least some transcendental conditionals should be understood as synthetic a posteriori, contra most thinkers in this area.

But now the crucial problem emerges: if transcendental conditionals are necessary, don't we have a case of *de re* necessity in Kripke's sense? But isn't that controversial? In the remainder of this section, we will make a case for thinking that some transcendental conditionals should be regarded as synthetic *de re* necessity statements. It is indeed controversial, and we will not pretend that it is a plain claim.

Let's have a brief look of Kripke's picture, though we will not provide a comprehensive description and defence of it. His case is primarily based on considerations from philosophy of language. For Kripke, proper names and natural kind terms are 'rigid designators' in that they refer to the same objects in all metaphysical possible worlds. Given that, statements such as 'water is H_2O' is necessary, since both 'water' and 'H_2O' are natural kind terms: these two terms refer to exactly the same substance in every metaphysically possible world. To be sure, other possible worlds might use different terms or spellings; some of them might not even have anything like the English language. The claim is that *our* terms refer to the same objects in *other* worlds. This picture is controversial for many reasons: it might be pointed out that strictly speaking, for chemical reasons, 'water is H_2O' is false; it might also be argued that there is no such thing as rigid designation. And there are many other objections in the literature. To be focussed, let's have a deeper look at considerations about rigid designation.

First of all, it might not be clear that notions in transcendental conditionals do involve rigid designators. Consider again our toy example (Sections 2.1 and

3.1): are 'objective cognition' and 'categories' rigid designators? They are certainly not proper names, but are they natural kind terms? Perhaps they are. How to delineate natural kinds is indeed disputed, but one might argue that both form distinctive kinds, and both are obviously natural. If so, then one needs to deal with all the extant problems with rigid designations. But one might instead hold that objective cognition and Kantian categories are too different from canonical natural kind cases such as water and tiger, so they are actually not natural kind terms. In that case, one cannot hold that those transcendental conditionals are *de re* necessity statements due to rigid designation. The good news is that one then need not worry about objections against rigid designation, but what would be the ground for thinking that those conditionals are *de re* necessity statements?

Although transcendental conditionals are not identity statements such as 'water is H_2O', let's consider the spirit behind rigid designation. Why is such a statement supposed to exemplify *de re* necessity? The idea is that in empirical worlds there are necessary connections, contra Quine. Given how human lungs work, for example, the air *has to have* certain components so as to make respiration through human lungs possible (Stern and Cheng 2023). To understand human lungs and air takes empirical studies, but that does not mean that there is no necessary connection between them. There are many similar examples one can come up with. Now are these necessary connections *logical* connections? It is unclear how considerations from logic are of any relevance here. Are they *nomological* connections? Since they are connections in natural worlds, they should qualify as nomological necessity. But are they also *metaphysical* necessity? This is hard to say. One might hold that given how human lungs work, if metaphysical laws work differently in certain possible worlds, perhaps we should conclude that those connections are not metaphysically necessary. But metaphysical laws are something philosophers have been struggling with. If one is not sure about metaphysical necessity, one can always retreat to nomological necessity, though the philosophical significance of that would decrease quite a bit. In what follows we will tentatively stick to the hypothesis that, at least in some cases, transcendental conditionals exemplify metaphysical necessity, and it is *de re* necessity in Kripke's sense.

It is illuminating to compare Kantian synthetic a priori with Kripkean *de re* necessity. On the one hand they are quite different: The former involves a *semantic* notion, while the latter concerns a *metaphysical* notion. But, on the other hand, they are similar in spirit in that they both embody the idea that certain statements have both traditional philosophical significance (being either a priori or necessary) and empirical relevance (being either synthetic or a posteriori). It is this latter spirit that the current hypothesis wishes to capture:

although one might hold dear to the picture that philosophy has its special place in all disciplines, contra Quine, one might also hope to make sure that philosophy is, or at least can be, about the empirical/natural worlds. Both the Kantian and the Kripkean ideas are very controversial, and perhaps none of them is defensible. However, it is the kind of enterprise that is worth pursuing: philosophy should stay special, but also relevant as well.

At this point, one might wonder what role the discussion of Kripke is really playing here. Is it just to show that there is a space to make claims that are metaphysically necessary yet synthetic a posteriori? Or is it also giving us a paradigm of the 'part of the essence of' relation? To answer this, I wish to emphasise that my claim is stronger than the idea that there is a theoretical space for us to try out: it is the more substantive claim that, at least in some cases, Kripkean *de re* necessity is a suitable model for us to understand transcendental conditionals. Relatedly, the Kripkean picture gives us a way to understand *essence*, and this is also a substantive point, as there are many competitors in the literature (e.g., Lewis 1986; Fine 1994). These substantive and controversial claims are directly relevant to transcendental conditionals because there are questions about whether they are a priori or a posteriori, and what kind of necessity is involved. It is a problem of the extant literature that the Kripkean picture is not in view at all. The major purpose of this section in particular, and of this Element in general, is to raise awareness that the Kripkean alternative should be taken seriously in the context of transcendental arguments and epistemology.[16]

Now we have arrived at our tentative hypothesis that at least some transcendental conditionals should be understood as synthetic *de re* necessity claims, or necessary a posteriori. We acknowledge that this is controversial and hard to defend, but we have also seen that it might be worth a try. One key point to be emphasised is that most other discussions in this Element are independent of the current hypothesis. The major reason why we put forward such a bold hypothesis is to guarantee the polemical nature of philosophical discussions, but even if it turns out to be false, we can still learn much along the way. Therefore we will stick to it and proceed. The next subsection will be about a specific explanatory notion, 'possibilitation', and we will introduce some considerations from contemporary modal epistemology and meta-metaphysics to illuminate our understanding of transcendental arguments.

3.3 Possibilitation

There are many characteristics of transcendental arguments, but a key one seems to be that they need to be *explanatory*. Consider our toy example again

---

[16] I thank a reviewer for urging me to be clearer here.

(Sections 2.1 and 3.1): Kantian categories are not only necessary conditions for objective cognition; they are supposed to explain *how objective cognition is possible* (contra Cassam 2007). But what kind of explanation is it? To get this clear, consider a non-transcendental condition:

Necessarily, being a dog requires or presupposes being a mammal.

We should all agree that there is *nothing transcendental* about it. Also, it should be an analytic statement. However, it seems to exemplify a certain kind of *explanatory* relation: something being a mammal at least partially explains something being a dog. In this case, given that it is an analytic statement, this should be taken as a *semantic* explanation: it is the kind of matter we can figure out through checking suitable dictionaries. By contrast, our transcendental conditionals, being synthetic, exemplify non-semantic explanations.

What kind of explanation is it, then? Since we hold the canonical view that transcendental arguments are designed to answer philosophical how-possible questions, *pace* Cassam (2007), we dub this kind of explanation 'possibilitation'. But giving it a name is not enough to substantiate it. In what follows we briefly consider what this kind of explanation might be.

It is instructive to further compare it with other kinds of explanations we know of. First of all, we have seen that it is no *semantic* explanation. Second, it is not *scientific* explanations we are familiar with: if it were, they would be indistinguishable from other empirical statements. As argued, some transcendental conditionals are *de re* necessity claims, which are partly philosophical and partly empirical, so scientific explanations do not fit the bill. What about *epistemic* explanations? Although we will soon consider modal epistemology, it is not quite right to regard possibilitation as epistemic. The reason is that, as argued in the previous subsection, the relations exemplified in those transcendental conditionals are presumably *metaphysical* ones, or at least nomological ones. Neither of them is epistemic in nature. In keeping with the hypothesis concerning metaphysical necessity, here we submit that possibilitation is a certain kind of *metaphysical* explanation.

But what kind of metaphysical explanation? There are some obvious candidates. *Supervenience* was prominent in the late twentieth century, but now the consensus seems to be that it is too weak to be a useful meta-metaphysical notion. There are obvious relations to be ruled out: Again, to use our toy example, it seems wrong to say that (the possibility of) objective cognition is *identical* to, *reducible* to, or *constituted* by Kantian categories. So there is not much left at our disposal. One natural remainder is *grounding*, which has generated many heated discussions in recent years. Intuitively, grounding is a kind of 'in virtue of' relation. For example, if we think chemical facts are grounded in physical facts, then chemical facts obtain *in virtue of* the grounding in physical facts. In our toy example, perhaps it can be said that facts about objective cognition are grounded in facts about Kantian categories. This reading seems intelligible on its face,[17] but there might be some concerns about whether possibilitation is a version of grounding.

To begin our criticisms of the grounding construal, in this way of paraphrasing or understanding transcendental conditionals, 'the possibility of' is missing. Relatedly, while grounding is a 'make-it-*the-case*' relation, possibilitation is a 'make-it-*possible*' relation. In this sense, possibilitation is more fundamental, as for something to be the case, it must first be possible. Possibilitation is thus conceptually prior to grounding. Moreover, here again we can see that first-order modal logic is too coarse-grained to capture either of these relations. Consider the following two statements:

Necessarily, facts about the brain *ground* facts about the mind.

Necessarily, Kantian categories *possibilitate* objective cognition.

While the former should have the conditional arrow from left to right (i.e., from brain to mind), the latter should have the conditional arrow from right to left (i.e., from objective cognition to Kantian categories) (for more on this, see Cheng in press). This is not a criticism of the two relations; nor is it a criticism of first-order modal logic. Rather, it is simply the claim that such a logic is not fine-grained enough to capture either of the relations. This reflects the general lesson in meta-metaphysics that while modal logic might be able to capture supervenience, it is unable to capture grounding. The takeaway message here is that *possibilitation* should be taken seriously by analytic metaphysics: along with identity, reduction, constitution, supervenience, grounding, and so forth, possibilitation is a relation that might obtain between properties, facts, substances, or phenomena. It is not something only of interest to those studying the history of Western philosophy, such as German idealism. Although the nature of possibilitation as explanatory needs further exploration, we tentatively propose that it is non-reductive and also non-constitutive. It is also not implicative inference, because it is not a kind of semantic relation.

Now why is modal epistemology relevant here? Recall that we tentatively hypothesise that some transcendental conditionals embody metaphysical necessity, and modal epistemology is a subdiscipline in philosophy that discusses how people go about figuring out the truth values of modal statements such as 'philosophical zombies are metaphysically (im)possible', 'twin earth is

---

[17] See, for example, C.-R. Yang, The Conditional Relation of Transcendental Arguments and Metaphysical Grounding (unpublished paper).

metaphysically (im)possible', 'inverted spectrum is metaphysically (im)possible', and so on. Very broadly, the positions can be divided into rationalism and empiricism. Within the rationalist camp, one prominent view is the so-called conceivability approach (Yablo 1993; Chalmers 1996, 2002). In broad strokes, it might propose using the following statement to figure out whether our toy example is metaphysically possible or not:

It is *inconceivable* that there is objective cognition without there being categories in place.

The basic idea is that conceivability is a certain kind of *evidence for* metaphysical possibility, while inconceivability is a certain kind of *evidence for* metaphysical impossibility. There are two caveats here. First, there is a stronger version, that the relation between (in)conceivability and (im)possibility is *entailment*, but it is safer to go with the weaker version invoking evidential support (cf. Mizrahi 2017, as discussed). Second, the two claims are logically independent of each other, though they often go hand in hand. Now the key point is that if it is metaphysically necessary that if P then Q, then it is *not* metaphysically possible there is P without Q. To follow the conceivability approach is certainly one way to understand how we can go about understanding and verifying statements of metaphysical possibility, but a natural worry is that all the problems that plague the conceivability approach would presumably plague this way of understanding transcendental conditionals, too. One can then try another view within rationalism, the 'essentialist approach' (Fine 1994; Lowe 2008, 2012). According to this idea, we may propose to use the following statement to figure out whether our toy example is metaphysically possible or not:

It is *part of the essence* of objective cognition that if there is objective cognition, then categories are in place.

Again, this approach might have some intuitive appeal, but it is not without its problems.

We can then turn to a rather different camp, empiricism, and see how things would look from that framework. One version of the view is the 'counterfactual approach' (Williamson 2007, 2016). According to this idea, we may propose to use the following statement to figure out whether our toy example is metaphysically possible or not:

If there *were* objective cognition without there being categories in place, then there *would be* a contradiction.

Such an approach is coupled with 'imaginative simulation' to render the inference intelligible. Williamson (2013) also argues that this is a kind of 'armchair knowledge', which is neither a priori nor a posteriori. It is doubtful, though, whether there can be this middle way. In the armchair, a philosopher can do purely a priori reflections or a posteriori empirical thinking. It seems that the dichotomy is firmly in place, and whether it is done by armchair discussions is beside the point. There are similar proposals in the literature (Kannisto 2020), and all of these approaches are worthy of further considerations.

Model epistemology is a rich area to be explored, and to be connected to our investigations into the nature of transcendental arguments. There are other approaches; for example, the one that relies on analogical inferences (Roca-Royes 2017). There are also mixed views such as 'imaginative variation' in Husserl (1931/1977) that unifies conceivability and essence into a single rationalist picture. These ideas might also be useful for us in figuring out what Kant, Fichte, Hegel, and others have in mind when invoking such an argument: Although there is always a danger of 'reading too much' into the history, it can also be illuminating to see whether contemporary approaches help us see more clearly the original insights from figures in our history.

Now, there might be a worry that possibilitation is merely defined negatively, that is, it is *not* grounding. Does it really do any significant work here? In response to this, consider its parallel notion, *necessitation*. Although it sounds as if it must be a *necessary* relation, things are not that straightforward. In his seminal work *Physicalism*, Daniel Stoljar (2010) critically discusses the question whether necessitation is itself a necessary relation. This is very significant because, for example, necessitation is often invoked to define supervenience, which is another vital notion in meta-metaphysics. Moreover, the importance of necessitation and supervenience goes beyond physicalism, as ethics and aesthetics also make use of such notions. Now, correspondingly, there are questions about whether possibilitation is necessary, and whether it is a priori, and so on. Just like the Kripkean picture discussed in the previous subsection, possibilitation is also missing in the literature on transcendental arguments in particular, and in meta-metaphysics more generally. It is true that in this Element we have not provided a complete logic and semantics for possibilitation, but it is to be insisted that it is a useful notion for the reasons provided, and it is certainly not a mere wordplay. How to substantiate this meta-metaphysical notion in a way that coheres with Kripkean essentialism is a topic for future research. There are many remaining questions here; for example, must possibilitation go with the Kripkean picture? Does this relation work better for *modest* transcendental arguments? How do we make sense of the idea that some facts in the objective world possibilitate one's mental faculties?

4 Transcendental Arguments in Action: The Revisionary Hypothesis Applied

In Section 3, we put forward a hypothesis about what (some) transcendental arguments should be: specifically, the relevant transcendental conditionals should be construed as synthetic necessary a posteriori statements. Assuming that is the right model for thinking about some transcendental claims, one would want to see how the model would work in actual examples. In this section we will consider three such examples. They are all claims in epistemology, which reflects the fact that this is an Element on transcendental *epistemology*, understood as answering epistemological how-possible questions. That said, let's not forget that even if some other examples are not themselves claims in epistemology, transcendental arguments should be taken as *epistemological* methods that help us achieve some specific argumentative goals.

4.1 McDowell's Case for Epistemological Disjunctivism

John McDowell has relied heavily on transcendental arguments throughout his career, though he has not always made this explicit. Most prominently, he invokes this strategy in the following three cases:

The possibility of intentionality requires the content view.
The possibility of intentionality requires conceptualism.
The possibility of intentionality requires epistemological disjunctivism.

To be sure, McDowell's writings are almost never straightforward, and often take lots of stage settings. In previous work, for example, Cheng (2021), I have conducted scholarly discussions of McDowell's convoluted dialectics. In this context, we will work with simplified versions of his ideas in order to focus on transcendental arguments. To begin with, the *actuality* of intentionality is affirmed. Now, with the obstacle-dependent approach (Cassam 2007), we can ask, for example, how is intentionality possible, *given physicalism*? McDowell holds that physicalism seems to make intentionality impossible, so a more relaxed naturalism is needed (McDowell 1996). But that is not enough. He goes further, to argue that the possibility of intentionality requires the content view, that is, the view that perceptual experiences have representational contents (Siegel 2010; Schellenberg 2011, 2018). The idea is that rational relations can *only* obtain between representational contents, so if perceptual experiences can have rational relations with judgements, those experiences must be contentful in the relevant sense, otherwise one commits the so-called Myth of the Given. This, to be sure, can be disputed (Travis 2006). Even further, McDowell (1996) argues that to avoid the Myth of the Given and make intentionality possible, conceptualism is required, that is, the view that the representational contents of perceptual experiences are *all conceptual*. This, again, has been heatedly disputed (Peacocke 1998, 2001). In what follows, we will focus on McDowell's similar argumentative moves in the realm of epistemology.

'Disjunctivism' is one of the most discussed labels in recent philosophy of mind and perception. There have been different taxonomies on offer (e.g., Byrne and Logue 2008; Haddock and Macpherson 2008), and it is difficult to come up with a framework that is accepted in the literature by most people. Without going into those details, here we begin with a simple distinction between the good case and the bad case (Williamson 2000). The *good* cases refer to veridical perceptions as we normally understand them. The *bad* cases refer to illusions, hallucinations, and various experiences of brains-in-vats (BIVs). For simplicity, let's focus on BIVs. Now, I am sitting at my desk and writing the draft of this section. My BIV counterpart would think and feel that he is also sitting at his desk and writing this section. Our experiences are *subjectively indistinguishable*. Does this mean that we share *exactly the same* conscious phenomenology? Some think 'yes' (Robinson 1994), others demur (Martin 2006). For those who deny this, they hold *phenomenal* or *experiential* disjunctivism. What about representational contents? Do my BIV counterpart and myself share the same representational contents? Again, for those who deny this, they hold *content* disjunctivism. Now, we can ask: do my BIV counterpart and myself share *the same evidence*? If one thinks not, then one holds *epistemological* disjunctivism. Why would anyone think so? Let's look into some details of McDowell's reasoning here.

Although McDowell has much to say about epistemology, he thinks that issues about intentionality and meaning are more fundamental than issues about knowledge and justification. The reason is simple: knowledge, justification, and the like all presuppose representational contents. Contents can be true or false, justified or unjustified, and so on. Therefore McDowell identifies a dominant way of thinking in Western philosophy that seems to make intentionality impossible: the so-called 'Cartesian inner space' (McDowell 1982, 1995). Within that inner psychological space, the subject's access to her/his mental episodes is completely secured, since it is *internal*. But there is a significant trade-off: the subject would have no direct access to the world *external* to her/him. According to this model, veridical perceptions, illusions, and hallucinations all share a *mental core*, which is perfectly knowable by the subject. Beyond that, whether one has (indirect) access to the external world would have to depend on how cooperative the world is, so to speak. In Williamson's terms, the subject in the good case and its counterpart in the bad case can in principle share the same evidence – *phenomenal* evidence, that is. As indicated, BIVs can make the picture vivid. Suppose I am lucky enough to be a normal human being, and I am not deceived by evil demons and so forth. I am revising this manuscript with my laptop in a cafe. My counterpart BIV also thinks he is sitting in this specific cafe, and revising this manuscript with this specific laptop. According to the inner-space model, my BIV counterpart and myself share *exactly the same experiential evidence*, since from the first-person point of view, it is indistinguishable who is in the good case, and who is in the bad case. Such a picture has various different names in the literature: common kind assumption, common element view, and so on. Standardly, sense-datum theorists (e.g., Robinson 1994) and representationalism/intentionalism (e.g., Byrne 2001) tend to commit to this picture, though conceptually they do not have to.

Now, McDowell's objection against the inner-space model roughly goes like this: there is no decisive reason to think that it is definitely wrong about us, but if it were the right model, intentionality would be impossible, as we would *never* be in any direct contact with the world. If we agree that we can at least *sometimes* think about the world, we are obliged to think that the good case and the bad case do not share that mental core. But our current topic is epistemology, so we cannot stop here just yet. McDowell further argues that the subject in the good case and its counterpart in the bad case do not share *the same evidence*: I am lucky enough to be a normal human being, so I have much better perceptual evidence than my BIV counterpart does. The key point is that subjective indistinguishability is *compatible* with such disjunctivism: we do not need to deny that in principle we cannot be sure we are in the good case or the bad case. Crucially, the fact that it takes *epistemic luck* to be in the good case does not show that the subject in the good case has no good evidence. To think otherwise is to demand that the subject must know too much in order to have any knowledge, and this high demand leads to unreasonable scepticism. The picture McDowell (and Williamson) is recommending is that we should embrace *epistemic luck* and not think that it needs to be entirely excluded in order to have evidence and knowledge. Consider this analogy in athletics: setting aside determinism, both how *good* the players are and how *lucky* they are play crucial roles in the results of games. Luck simply cannot be ruled out in such situations. The same can be said about many other human activities, such as job hunting and leading happy lives. If we do not have to rule out luck in all other human achievements, why think that in *epistemic* achievements there is any difference?

As acknowledged at the start of this subsection, McDowell scholarship is not the point here. What is important in this context is to see his epistemological disjunctivism and the relevant transcendental argument. We have seen that McDowell's primary concern is intentionality, so he begins with the *actuality* of intentionality as one crucial premise. Now, for the relevant transcendental conditional, epistemological disjunctivism is said to be a transcendental condition of possibility for intentionality. If we follow the Kripkean *de re* necessity line, we should say that epistemological disjunctivism is *part of the essence* of intentionality. But this sounds very strange: does it even make sense to think that a theory is part of the essence of something else? How should we proceed here?

Note that in one of our toy examples in Sections 2.1 and 3.1, Kantian categories are said to be part of the essence of objective cognition. There was no such problem there. In the present context, epistemological disjunctivism amounts to the claim of *the factivity of evidence*: If I am lucky enough to be a normal human being enjoying veridical perceptual experiences, I then have the relevant *factive* evidence, which is not accessible by my BIV counterpart. Therefore, we can say that *the factivity of evidence* is part of the essence of intentionality: The possibility of intentionality requires that evidence is factive, not phenomenal. Of course, this is a simplified way of putting the idea, and it can look misleading, but at least we have some good ideas about how the relevant transcendental conditional might work in McDowell's case for epistemological disjunctivism.

It is not hard to apply our hypothesis to McDowell's transcendental conditionals. Let's stick to the example. Suppose the possibility of intentionality requires or presupposes the factivity of evidence. This is not established solely by conceptual analysis, and one needs to consider all kinds of cases in the empirical world. Therefore, it is sensible to say that the conditional is synthetic and necessary a posteriori. Whether one wishes to accept such a conditional, to be sure, is quite a different matter.

Are McDowell's transcendental arguments moderate or ambitious? Since the content view and conceptualism are about one's own mind, these two are *self-directed* and therefore moderate. What about the one for disjunctivism? Since it is about factivity and the world, it seems to be *world-directed* and ambitious. Does it mean that this final one is more problematic in this respect? Here, it is crucial to bear in mind that McDowell has a very special ontology of the world, which is often ignored in the analytic literature. For him, there is a Gadamerian distinction between the *environment* and the *world* (Gadamer 1960/1989). While the former roughly equals the physical world as understood by most philosophers, the Gadamerian world and the human mind are mutually dependent. Given this ontology, McDowell's transcendental argument concerning disjunctivism is actually less ambitious than it seems: it is similar to Kant's case and although Kant also makes claims about the world via transcendental arguments, given his transcendental idealism, the claims about the world are actually not that ambitious. Although McDowell is no transcendental idealist, he is a certain kind of idealist given the commitment to the Gadamerian world. Here, we do not defend such an ontology, but just point out that McDowell's transcendental argument for disjunctivism is a peculiar one given his special ontology (Cheng 2021). Note that Keith Allen (2017) has proposed so-called 'transcendental naïve realism', which, since he does not share McDowell's peculiar ontology, involves *ambitious* transcendental arguments. It is worth exploring how convincing Allen's case is for such an ambitious project.[18]

4.2 Cassam's Case for Epistemological Objectivism

Although Cassam's (1997) *Self and World* and McDowell's (1996) *Mind and World* engage similar dialectics, and both are Kantian in flavour, somehow the former has not generated too much attention. However, it is a carefully written work which is full of insights. In this section, we will focus on his case for a certain view about bodily self-awareness and, as we shall see, more than one transcendental argument is invoked.

First of all, what is epistemological objectivism? To see this, some stage setting is required. Wittgenstein (1914–1916: 80) once remarked that 'The I is not an object.' Although Wittgenstein himself would presumably disown any philosophical labels, this view has been called 'anti-objectivism' by others (Sluga 1996). And given that the view is about the nature of the self, it is apt to call it 'metaphysical anti-objectivism'. Not surprisingly, we will focus here on its epistemic counterpart, 'epistemological anti-objectivism', which is about *self-awareness* or consciousness: The subject is not, or cannot, be aware of itself as an object. Another name for this negative idea is the 'elusiveness thesis' (Cassam 1995). So epistemological objectivism is anti-elusive in holding that the subject *can* be aware of itself as an object. One might think, 'who would object to *that*?'. According to Cassam, at least, it is incompatible with this Humean idea:

> 'When I enter most intimately into what I call myself, I always stumble on some particular perception or other . . . I can never catch myself without a perception, and can never observe anything but the perception.' (Hume 1739/1978) T 1.4.6.3, SBN 252

In our era, Sydney Shoemaker (1984: 102; emphases rearranged) argues that 'when one is *introspectively* aware of one's thoughts, feelings, beliefs and desires, one is not presented to oneself as a flesh and blood person, and does not seem to be presented to oneself as an *object* at all'. Hume and Shoemaker's ideas provide

---

[18] I thank a reviewer for pressing me on this point concerning the nature of McDowell's argument.

a clear background against which Cassam develops his epistemological objectivism – though we will not go into detail about why they would think so.

Cassam's (1997) argumentations in *Self and World* are very complicated; here is a brief summary. In order to establish his claim, Cassam offers two main lines of argumentation: One is the Unity Argument plus the Objectivity Argument; and the other is the Identity Argument. The Unity Argument holds that for one to be self-conscious, one must be capable of self-ascribing various experiences at different times, which in turn requires the unity of consciousness and subsequently the objectivity condition, that is, a capacity for being 'in a position to conceptualize one's perceptions as perceptions of objects in the weighty sense' (Cassam 1997: 31). The Objectivity Argument has it that the objectivity condition requires 'awareness of oneself, *qua* subject of experience, as a physical object' (Cassam 1997: 28; 'the materialist conception'). The Unity Argument plus the Objectivity Argument form a long train of thought from self-consciousness to the materialist conception, that is, the anti-elusiveness claim. After his extensive and intricate discussions of versions of the Unity Argument and the Objectivity Argument, Cassam concludes that the line of argumentation has not adequately established the intended conclusion. Therefore, he moves to the Identity Argument, and specifically argues that, ultimately, only the *intuition* version of this argument works: 'Consciousness of one's own identity as the subject of different representations requires intuitive awareness of oneself as a physical object' (Cassam 1997: 118). And this is required by self-consciousness. Thus, Cassam concludes that the intuition version of the Identity Argument is successful in repelling the Humean Elusiveness Thesis.[19]

Now in order to be focussed, let's consider the Objectivity Argument only. What is the objectivity condition? In this context, the condition is about the possibility of objective experience, and objectivity here means 'existence when unperceived' (Strawson 1959). Here, Cassam argues that the possibility of objective experience, that is, the possibility of experiencing something as existing when unperceived, requires or presupposes that one can be aware of oneself qua experiential subject as a physical object. According to our conception of transcendental conditionals, this statement is a synthetic one: it is not simply true in virtue of meaning. It is a posteriori in that in order to establish it, empirical considerations are required. It is also necessary in that the kind of self-awareness is a necessary condition for the possibility of objective experience.

What does Cassam mean by 'qua subject' here? When one sees a mirror, one might be aware of oneself as a physical object – one sees a body that is identical to oneself – but it is possible that one is not aware of it qua subject, since subject

---

[19] I used this outline in my dissertation (Cheng 2018) and in Cheng (2021).

in the relevant sense can experience and act, and when seeing oneself in a mirror, there is no guarantee that one is aware of oneself in such a first-person way. In order to become aware of oneself qua subject, it seems necessary that one is aware of oneself *from the inside*: one is aware of oneself *introspectively*, as it is usually put. Now, assuming this line of thought is roughly correct, it is not reached by conceptual analysis only: it is not as if we analyse the concept of a mirror and the concept of a body and so on and obtain the conclusion. Also, considering such cases is not a matter of a priori endeavour: Although we do not go about doing experiments on it, it is different in kind from mathematics and logic. This is relevant to Williamson's discussions of apriority, aposteriority, and armchair. Again, my view is that things are either a priori or a posteriori, and being armchair is not the same as being a priori: scientists conduct all kinds of empirical discussions and make all kinds of empirical predictions in lab meetings, but those are obviously a posteriori and empirical matters. In considering the mirror case, Cassam is, among other things, in effect rendering the conditional a posteriori, even though he does not put things in this way.

It is instructive at this point to consider a general objection to this kind of project, as it is almost always regarded as a priori and therefore hopeless. Here is a passage from an empirical Kantian, Andrew Brook (2001: 190), who is opposing 'the Kantian tradition that grew out of P. F. Strawson's work at Oxford in the 1960s':

> Oxford Kantianism insists upon a deep divide between philosophy and empirical psychology . . . This insistence is peculiar. Philosophers make claims about the mind, specifically, about how the mind must be . . . Surely it cannot be a matter of indifference whether the mind actually is as they claim it to be. Nor is it always clear what is being contrasted to empirical psychology.

After this, Brook goes on to point out that, according to Cassam (1997: 83), the contrast here is between the empirical and the transcendental. The first thing to note is that although the later Cassam (2007) regards transcendental arguments as *irrelevant* to answering philosophical how-possible questions, his attitude towards empirical considerations is the same: he is not against sciences at all, though in his own works empirical considerations are almost never explicit. Now, Brook seems to assume that as long as people do not build their cases on empirical considerations, the results are exclusively a priori. But this is exactly what I wish to oppose: what Cassam has been doing is armchair philosophy for sure, but it does not follow that his discussions are a priori. Going back to our case, the transcendental conditional in question is established partially by considering the mirror case, which is different in kind from mathematics and logic. Brook can be dissatisfied with Cassam's science-free method, but to criticise it on the grounds of its being a priori seems to miss the mark. If the major hypothesis in this Element is correct, at least some transcendental conditionals, including the one we are considering in this section, are necessary a posteriori. It might be better to incorporate insights from empirical sciences, but failing to do so does not render the results a priori.

David Papineau (2003) has offered a slightly different criticism of John Campbell (2002), specifically targeting his *Reference and Consciousness*. Here is Papineau (2003: 12):

> This modern neo-Kantianism has been enormously influential within Oxford, and is establishing notable outposts elsewhere in the English-speaking world ... Throughout most of the twentieth century, academic philosophy organized itself around the great fault-line dividing the 'Continental' and 'analytic' schools ... Oxford neo-Kantianism has added a new ingredient to the philosophical mix ... [A] new and potentially more fruitful division is emerging within English-speaking philosophy. In place of the old analytic–Continental split, we now have the opposition between the naturalists and the neo-Kantians. The naturalists look to science to provide the starting point for philosophy. The neo-Kantians start with consciousness instead.

Papineau continues to criticise neo-Kantianism for ignoring the sciences. The spirit is basically the same as Brook's (2001) criticism. I do not agree with Papineau's criticism here, as Campbell (2002) obviously takes the relevant sciences seriously, not only in *Reference and Consciousness* but also in other works. In any case, we can have the same reply here: even if Cassam and Campbell – and McDowell for that matter – do not always invoke scientific considerations in their works, it does not mean that those aspects of their works are a priori. As another philosopher who often implicitly uses Kantian transcendental method, Campbell's relevant claims are also often synthetic necessary a posteriori. There will be more on the relation between transcendental projects and scientific projects in Section 5.[20]

4.3 Smithies's Case for Phenomenal Accessibilism

Declan Smithies' take on epistemology is distinctive in that it combines considerations about *consciousness* with issues in epistemology. Of course, he is not the only one who does so – Fred Dretske, Susanna Siegel, Nicholas Silins, and

---

[20] Before 2007 or thereabouts, Cassam's works are full of transcendental conditionals, or something close enough. For example, he has argued that 'awareness of one's own body is a necessary condition for the acquisition and possession of concepts of primary qualities such as force and shape' (Cassam 2002: 315). He also discusses the existence/idea/perception of space as necessary for objective experience (Cassam 2005), and connects these views to Kant, Strawson, and Evans. Note that in those discussions he often does not state 'the possibility of', but it does not mean that those statements should not be interpreted in that way.

Susanna Schellenberg are notable examples – but his particular approach could be a good example for us because it has a certain transcendental flavour, even if Smithies himself does not state things in transcendental terms. To begin with, some have argued that consciousness has no obvious function (Rosenthal 2008), while others hold that consciousness has clear functions and causal powers, at least in humans (Dretske 1997). Smithies follows this latter line, and argues for an even stronger view that consciousness in humans like us has a *unique* function: It makes justification and knowledge possible. It is unique in that its role cannot be replaced by any other items. In our terms, consciousness *possibilitates* justification and knowledge. From this, we can already see that Smithies' project is transcendental, but there is more to explore. In what follows, we selectively go into the details of aspects of his transcendental epistemic project.[21]

Smithies usefully labels his theses clearly, and provides clear definitions. For example, he holds 'phenomenal mentalism': 'Necessarily, which propositions you have epistemic justification to believe at any given time is determined solely by your phenomenally individuated mental states at that time' (Smithies 2019: 25).

And he also holds 'accessibilism': 'Necessarily, if it is evidently probable that p to degree n, then it is evidently certain that it is evidently probable that p to degree n' (Smithies 2019: 219). Putting these ideas together results in his 'phenomenal accessibilism', which is a specific version of internalism about justification. One notable point here is that in formulating his theses, Smithies almost always begins with 'necessarily'. This is important for at least two reasons. First, although many theses in philosophy are formulated as universal claims, like 'all knowledge is justified true beliefs', the spirit behind those theses actually involves *necessity*. This is why, for example, physicalists need to worry about metaphysically possible scenarios. It is a virtue of Smithies' writing that it makes this commitment to necessity explicitly. Second, and perhaps more importantly for our purposes, this necessity indicates the connection between Smithies' theses and transcendental philosophy. Although he argues for many ideas in *The Epistemic Role of Consciousness*, including the ones referred to, let's focus on the following, as it makes it very clear that Smithies (2019) is engaging in transcendental inquiries:

The possibility of perceptual justification requires or presupposes the presentational force of perceptual experience.

---

[21] In Smithies (2022), where he responds to my attempt here, he does not object to the idea of explicitly transcendentalising his project.

In Cheng (2022: 4), I dub this 'transcendental phenomenal internalism'. In Smithies' (2019: 74) chapter on perception, he writes that he aims 'to examine what perception must be like in order to play this justifying role', and it is not a stretch to reformulate this inquiry in transcendental terms. Now, applying our model of what transcendental arguments should be, at least in some cases, we should say that this thesis – so-called transcendental phenomenal internalism – is a synthetic statement: it is not true in virtue of meaning, if it is true at all. It is necessary in that it means, necessarily, perceptual justification requires or presupposes the presentational force of perceptual experience. Crucially, it is a posteriori, it is about the empirical worlds, including our world. Its truth, if true at all, is not like mathematical or logical truths. It relies on *both* conceptual analyses and empirical considerations, even if it does not involve experimental projects directly. In a Kripkean spirit, we can say that the presentational force of perceptual experience is part of the essence of perceptual justification, and perhaps of perceptual knowledge as well. Last but not least, the presentational force of perceptual experience *possibilitates* justification and knowledge: The former transcendentally explains the latter.

In this section, we saw three examples of transcendental arguments in epistemology. After explaining the basic ideas from the three authors, we applied our hypothesis to those arguments. It needs to be stressed that the hypothesis is not designed to capture those authors' intentions. Indeed, they might even object to such an interpretation. The purpose of the application is not to provide faithful interpretations of those ideas. Rather, it is to show how the hypothesis *could* work with extant examples in the literature. It is important to see that although the hypothesis and those materials are independent of one another, they seem to sit well. Even if those authors might not approve of such interpretations, and even if the proposed hypothesis might not be workable, I hope readers will still learn something important along the way.

5 Roads Ahead

In this concluding secton, we are now in a better position to see clearly the prospects of transcendental arguments in particular, and transcendental epistemology in general. Before exploring those prospects and addressing potential worries, let's first take stock. This Element began with an introduction to the subject of 'transcendental epistemology' in Section 1. We then looked into epistemological how-possible questions that define transcendental epistemology as a domain, and discussed Cassam's multi-levels response to those questions. After addressing Cassam's criticisms against transcendental arguments, at least tentatively, we gave a preliminary formulation of such arguments. Section 2 provided a brief historical overview of transcendental arguments, including those in Kant and the German idealists, phenomenologists, and analytic philosophers. Section 3 proposed the hypothesis that at least some transcendental conditionals should be understood as synthetic, necessary, and a posteriori statements. It ended by introducing a specific notion of transcendental explanation, 'possibilitation'. Section 4 put the hypothesis to work by considering three examples in (transcendental) epistemology: McDowell's case for epistemological disjunctivism, Cassam's case for epistemological objectivism, and Smithies' case for phenomenal accessibilism. The basic message has been that even if the hypothesis proposed here turns out to be wrong, which is quite likely given that most hypotheses in philosophy are wrong, readers could learn something from this intellectual journey. In this final section, we will first check whether transcendental arguments can be naturalised, and if so in what sense. We will then propose that there is an ineliminable transcendental level of analysis that goes with many philosophical questions. Finally, we will address the worry that although many (though not all) transcendental arguments are designed to meet sceptical challenges, this form of argumentation can potentially be invoked by some sceptics.

5.1 Can Transcendental Arguments Be Naturalised?

Before asking whether something can be naturalised, one should perhaps ask: why bother? Why do we want to naturalise, say, intentionality or consciousness? There is a standard answer to this: if the world is ultimately natural, to be defined in various ways, then only natural phenomena can be said to exist in this natural world. This is the *ontological* version of naturalism, and it makes sense to ponder whether phenomena such as intentionality and consciousness can be naturalised. Now, transcendental arguments are different: They are not phenomena or properties; rather, they belong to a certain kind of *method*. So in asking why transcendental arguments should be naturalised, and how we can go about naturalising them, we can focus on the *methodological* version of naturalism.

To make progress, let's consider another inferential method, logical deduction. There is nothing *unnatural* about it, one might say. But as a method should it be naturalised? If by this we mean whether it should emulate methods in the empirical sciences, the answer is perhaps 'no': logical deduction is a good method, but it is not supposed to be an empirical method. Sciences should not be the only measures of good methods. If anything is legitimately a priori, one might think, logical deduction is.

Now what about transcendental arguments? Note that according to the standard understanding provided in the SEP entry (Stern and Cheng 2023), which we have adopted with qualification, all transcendental arguments should be able to be reduced to two premises: the transcendental conditional, stating that the possibility of *Y* requires or presupposes *X*; and one that states that *Y* is actual and therefore possible.[22] This is why some have wondered whether there is any difference between transcendental arguments and *modus ponens*. Now, even if they are different, as we have seen in earlier sections, their forms are quite similar. One notable difference is that transcendental conditionals might not be deductive.[23] If so, then the considerations noted about logical deduction do not apply. So should, and can, transcendental arguments be naturalised?

The premise about the *actuality* of certain phenomena should not cause any problems here. For example, it might state that objective cognition is a genuine phenomenon in the actual world. Even if such a statement can be falsified, it is clear that it is about the *actual, empirical, natural* world. This is where ontological naturalism comes in. What about the conditional premise? As we have seen, most if not all philosophers working in this area believe transcendental arguments are a priori and, given this, it can seem difficult to see how such conditionals can be naturalised methodologically. However, if our hypothesis is right about some transcendental conditionals, they are in effect a posteriori, so at least they are or can be naturalised in principle.

Does this mean that this kind of transcendental method should be assimilated into *scientific or empirical* method? Definitely not. Recall that our general picture is Kripkean. Although Kripke uses a certain conceivability method to reach anti-naturalist dualism, we do not follow that path. Rather, we focus on the idea that what's being required or presupposed are *essences*: if we say the possibility of objective cognition requires or presupposes Kantian categories, then those categories are *part of the essence* of objective cognition. This is a claim about the actual world, and many other possible worlds too. Now, a potential worry is that if such conditionals are about all metaphysically possible worlds, but some of those possible worlds contain unnatural beings or phenomena, wouldn't this be a problem? Here, we need to note that, for the conditionals, the issue about whether they can be naturalised is *methodological*. Sticking to this idea, even if it is applied in unnatural worlds, the method itself can be natural. This verdict is controversial, and I must admit that it is not too clear whether this is really workable, or how important it is to worry about naturalisation. However, given the prominence of both ontological and

---

[22] Again, the 'self-conscious premise' in Tse (2020).

[23] As discussed, Kant certainly gives this impression in his wordings, but one wonders: if logical deduction is not what is at issue here, how can we sensibly talk about necessary conditions?

methodological naturalism in contemporary Western philosophy, whether a given method can be naturalised in any significant sense should be something we take seriously.

In his article Can Transcendental Epistemology be Naturalized?, Cassam (2003) directly tackles this question about naturalisation. He makes a distinction between *analytic* transcendental epistemology and *naturalised* transcendental epistemology (Cassam 2003: 203), and argues that the latter is problematic. However, he thinks that in naturalising transcendental epistemology, we commit to the 'dependency thesis' that 'a proper investigation of transcendentally necessary conditions must lean in important respects on the deliverances of science' (Cassam 2003: 181). As we have seen, our way of naturalising transcendental arguments and epistemology is *not* like that. In Cassam's discussions, Kripkean *de re* necessity is not in view. Without rehearsing the gist of the picture, here we hold that transcendental arguments and epistemology *can* be naturalised without collapsing them into sciences or scientific epistemology (Kornblith 2021).

So what exactly is the naturalisation question for transcendental arguments and epistemology? For Cassam, and perhaps for Brook and Papineau, the distinction seems to hinge on whether one is relying on empirical research. This is certainly one way to understand the question. However, another intelligible way to proceed is to acknowledge certain transcendental conditionals as a posteriori, and that to do this does not commit one to do cognitive sciences oneself. In Cassam (2007), for example, many considerations about the relation between object perceptions and spatial perceptions are blatantly a posteriori, but this does not mean that those considerations have to come from empirical studies. Again, taking cognitive sciences into account explicitly might help us make better progress, to be sure, but in naturalising transcendental arguments, it is not a requirement that the proponents themselves draw on empirical research. 'Methodological naturalism' here means that methods in the empirical sciences should be considered in the inquiries, but it does not mean that those who follow this doctrine needs to discuss those empirical methods and results themselves.[24]

5.2 Transcendental Level of Analysis

What are levels of analysis? Talk about levels are ubiquitous in philosophy, and people can mean different things by this term. The basic distinction is between levels of *existence* and levels of *analysis*, though there might be different labels for them. For the former, it has been argued by some that what there is in the world constitutes a *levelled* structure: physics, chemistry, biology, psychology,

---

[24] I thank a reviewer for pressing me on this.

economics, and so forth have their own levels of existence. If this is so, an urgent question concerns how these levels relate to one another. *Reductionisms* in the relevant sense tend not to accept such level talk. Standardly, ontological levels couple with a certain version of *emergentism*: chemistry emerges from physics, biology emerges from chemistry, and so on (O'Connor 2020). How, exactly, emergence should be defined is a matter of dispute, but the basic idea is that the emergent levels have *novel* properties: some chemical properties cannot be found at the physical level, some biological properties cannot be found at the chemical level, and so on. Since what concerns us here are levels of *analysis*, we shall not go into thorny matters about levels of *existence*.

Very generally, levels of analysis are epistemological: one can analyse the same set of phenomena from different angles, or at different levels. If one accepts levels of existence, one should definitely analyse those ontological levels with different levels of analysis: physical science analyses the ontological physical level, chemical science analyses the ontological chemical level, and so on. Crucially, even if one does not accept levels of *existence* – one might hold that ontologically speaking there is only one level – one can, and perhaps should, accept levels of *analysis*. Perhaps everything is ultimately physical, so ontologically speaking there is only one level, but this physical reality can be understood or analysed in different terms, so has different levels in the current sense. An example might help. Suppose I am an average human being sitting in a cafe. I exhibit some behaviours: I type, I read, I drink, and I look around. It is totally possible to analyse these behaviours in physical terms, especially if we assume that we already have complete and perfect physics. My behaviours can also be analysed in chemical terms (molecular biology), biological terms (evolutionary biology), psychological terms (empirical psychology), and every-day terms (folk psychology). Whether these latter terms should be reduced to physical terms is an issue we can leave open.

Now, how exactly these two concepts of levels – existence and analysis – interact with each other is complicated. Some have argued that levels of analysis can constrain levels of ontology – Dennett's (1989) intentional stance comes to mind (also see List 2019). Here, we adopt the conservative picture that there might or might not be levels of existence, but in any case, it makes sense to maintain different levels of analysis, as some levels might contain insights that are invisible at other levels. Now, if there is a *transcendental* level of analysis at all, we need to see what the other levels are, and how they interact. This is what we will focus on in the remainder of this section.

We can begin with the examples cited, that is, the common distinctions between physics, chemistry, biology, and psychology. In Kant, we see an attempt to look for foundations for empirical sciences. Given that his approach in philosophy is undoubtedly transcendental, and he does invoke transcendental arguments in our sense, we can see Kant as engaging in a specific version of *transcendental analysis*, which is distinct from other levels of analysis. Husserl engages in a similar project in the twentieth century. Nowadays, even if most of us do not believe in Kant's or Husserl's specific projects, it should not follow that such transcendental analyses are doomed to fail. That being said, it is true that finding foundations for sciences seems to reach a dead end, so we should avoid such an ambitious project.

As a result, the picture recommended here does not seek to provide any foundation for empirical sciences. The transcendental analysis is relevant to and will have an impact on sciences, but in a way that is weaker than providing foundations. Another difference is that although it is fine to stick to the levels of physics, chemistry, biology, psychology, and so forth, it might seem a bit too general to see how exactly they work in specific cases. Here, we will discuss a specific proposal from David Marr (1982), and see how our transcendental level of analysis can supplement and enrich Marr's already very useful levels. Simply stated, Marr's levels are as follows:

Computational Level: What does the system do? What problems does it solve or overcome?

Algorithmic or Representational Level: How does the system do what it does? What representations does it use, and what processes does it employ to build and manipulate those representations?

Implementational or Physical Level: How is the system physically realised or implemented?

Marr's primary concern is human visual systems, so it makes sense to speak of representations at the middle level. If one applies this framework to other domains, where representations are not involved, one needs to reformulate that second level. In what follows we stick to Marr's example, though we will extend it to other sense modalities as well. *What do the perceptual systems do?* They perceptually take in colours, contours, sounds, smells, and other external stimuli. What problems do they solve or overcome? There are many, but a famous one is about how the visual system computes the inverse retinal images so that what we see is not inverted. Another one is the binding problem that since processes for colours, shapes, and movements are done with different timings, how can the perceptual systems produce a coherent picture of the world for the perceivers? These questions are canonical ones in cognitive psychology. *How does the system do what it does?* This question can seem underspecified, but one can look into cognitive neuroscience and theoretical neuroscience for answers. The former studies neural representations and processes with neuroimaging techniques, while the latter applies mathematical methods to model human perceptual systems, among other things. As for *how the systems are physically realised or implemented*, one needs to go down to molecular biology, and also chemistry and physics, to figure out the exact implementations or realisation. 'Multiple realisability' comes in here, as the same algorithms might be able to be realised with different materials or different ways physically, at least in principle.

Now, why isn't this enough? Why do we need another level, that is, our *transcendental* level of analysis? Since we are using perception and human perceptual systems as examples, let's consider this:

Transcendental Level: How is it possible for the system to do what it does, *given specific obstacles* highlighted by (say) the argument from hallucination?

The brings us back to one of our starting points: philosophical how-possible questions are obstacle-dependent (Cassam 2007), and after the relevant obstacles are specified, one needs to either overcome or dissipate them. Here, our example is the argument from hallucination, so we will go into some detail. This example will also be used in our final subsection, so having some basic ideas about it will be helpful.

Terms such as 'illusions' and 'hallucinations' are commonly used in everyday English, and in empirical psychology too. In philosophy of perception, 'hallucinations' often refer to perceptual experiences that do not correspond to any relevant environmental objects and properties. For example, sitting in the cafe, I might suddenly hallucinate a pink elephant dancing on my left-hand side, but objectively speaking there is nothing to my left that corresponds to it. This can be controversial, as there is a table to my left, and who is to say that my relevant experience is *not* an illusion of that table? Also in philosophy of perception, 'illusions' often refer to the perceptual experiences that take in the objects successfully but get the properties wrong. Perhaps my relevant experience gets the properties of the table so wrong that it looks as if there is a pink elephant to my left. For our purposes, we do not engage in the business of drawing a theoretical line between illusions and hallucinations. We will stick to hallucinations, as the challenge from the argument from hallucination might be slightly easier to understand than the challenge from the argument from illusion.

Although there have been many formulations of the so-called argument from hallucination, it generally begins with the idea or premise that hallucinations are *possible*. As A. D. Smith (2002) emphasises, the argument does not need the reality or actuality of hallucinations. Mere possibility of hallucinations will do. Now in those possible hallucinations, what do we experience? In the example just given, the possible hallucination involves me experiencing a pink elephant dancing to my left. But there are no relevant properties or objects around that corner, so the most sensible thing to say, the thinking goes, is that in that possible hallucination I am experiencing *mental objects* – so-called sense-data – and those objects are different from external, physical objects. Now, two reasons have been put forward for the idea that if we grant this step, there is no way for us to prevent generalisations from possible hallucinations to other perceptual cases. The first reason is *subjective indiscriminability*: in principle, some possible hallucinations are subjectively or experientially indistinguishable from corresponding veridical experiences (see our earlier discussions of McDowell in Section 4). And given that conscious experiences are *subjective* phenomena, the fact that these experiences cannot be told apart from the subjects in question is enough to guarantee that if we perceive mental objects in possible hallucinations, then we perceive mental objects in *all* cases. The second reason focusses instead on *objective identical processes*, in this case our brain processes. Since the most proximal causes of our conscious experiences are the relevant brain processes, if those brain processes in the possible hallucinations produce experiences of mental objects, then the same brain processes should produce *exactly the same experiences* of mental objects, even if in the so-called veridical perception cases, there are corresponding properties and objects in the relevant parts of the environment.

This is an extremely compressed version of the argument and, as it stands, one might find it invalid or weak. In any serious discussion of this argument, it is formulated with multiple premises, sometimes four and often more, and defenders of it have tried hard to make sure it is a valid argument (Robinson 1994), though many have pointed out that none of the attempts so far have been successful (French and Walters 2018). For our purposes, though, this simple sketch is enough. The key point is that the argument from hallucination has set up a unique obstacle to the possibility of *perception*. More specifically, if we follow the common idea that perceptions should at least *sometimes* put us in touch with the external world, but now encounter the obstacle that given the possibility of hallucination perceptions *never* put us in touch with the world, then we need to figure out how it is possible for the perceptual systems to do what they do – putting us in touch with the external world – given threats from the argument from hallucinations, and perhaps other obstacles too.

We can think of the transcendental level and other levels as the two premises of canonical transcendental arguments. The computational, algorithmic, and implementational levels are about the *actual* perceptual processes. The transcendental level instead begins with the possibility of perceptions – perceptions are actual so they are possible – and ask what *possibilitates* perceptions, given the obstacles. The various responses to the argument from hallucination – adverbialism, intentionalism, disjunctivism, and so on – can be seen as providing such conditions of possibility. Although practitioners in philosophy of perception might not have thought of those issues in transcendental terms, it is certainly reasonable to reframe those traditional discussions in such terms. Recent examples can be found in Gomes (2017) and Allen (2017). In this way, the transcendental level of analysis supplements and enriches Marr's original levels. While perceptual scientists and some philosophers of perception care about how the perceptual systems *actually* work, there is something distinctive about what philosophy can do here: it can provide a transcendental level of analysis concerning *possibility* (cf. Burge 2010, 2022).

5.3 Scepticism Strikes Back

But now we face a potential problem: We have seen that there is a transcendental level of analysis that is about what the possibility of perceptions requires. As we have also seen in the previous sections, transcendental arguments are often, though not always, anti-sceptical. Now, if one instead begins with the possibility of *hallucinations*, as in the argument from hallucination, one might arrive at the conclusion that one can only perceive mental objects in all cases of perception, including veridical and non-veridical ones. But this seems wrong from the transcendental point of view: does it even make sense to think that one can invoke transcendental methods to argue for any form of scepticism?

To this, there are various potential responses. Those who defend the argument from hallucination could say that their conclusion is not scepticism per se, but sense-datum theories or indirect realism. Although their opponents often claim that such theories *will* collapse into scepticism, it does not mean that they *do* commit to scepticism of any sort. Moreover, even if they do lead to scepticism, it only means that transcendental arguments as argumentative forms can be invoked by anyone who believes in such arguments. Just like other inferential methods such as deduction, induction, and abduction, inferential methods or *forms* should be detached from the actual *contents* in those inferences.

It is understandable that most proponents of transcendental arguments cannot accept this consequence. We can envisage three reactions here:

A. Transcendental arguments *have to be* anti-sceptical.
B. Transcendental arguments are *often though not always* anti-sceptical.
C. Transcendental arguments are purely argumentative methods, so whether they are anti-sceptical is *entirely contingent or coincidental*.

Some Kant scholars might hold A, but it is arguable that *not all* of Kant's transcendental arguments are obviously anti-sceptical. A is even harder to defend if we agree that other philosophers have been invoking transcendental arguments for different purposes. Perhaps the distinction between regressive and progressive transcendental arguments is relevant here. In this Element we have adopted the moderate view, B, that such arguments are often though not always anti-sceptical. However, this view permits that the argument from hallucination *can* be regarded as a transcendental argument, and this might be unacceptable. One solution is to add a qualification:

B'. Transcendental arguments are often though not always anti-sceptical. However, they *can never* be sceptical.

This is indeed enough to rule out cases where sceptics use transcendental arguments to argue for their sceptical conclusions, but it seems uncomfortably ad hoc. However, C seems to be at odds with the basic spirit of transcendental arguments, so that is not the way to go. What should we do now?

This is actually a difficult question that I would like to leave open for readers to ponder. It is possible that no easy way out is forthcoming, but how damaging this will be for the prospects of transcendental arguments is also unclear. The picture recommended here is that we can and should be less worried about scepticism, and just focus on how good the relevant arguments are. If some sceptics can make good use of any argument for their conclusions, then so be it. What is more important is that we examine those arguments and say where they go wrong. If we worry so much about scepticism that we want to stipulate that certain arguments cannot be invoked by them, the resulting picture might be hopelessly ad hoc and unfair to our sceptical opponents.

This somewhat dim observation concludes our intellectual journey through transcendental arguments and transcendental epistemology. Obviously, everything said here is far from the last word, and many significant discussions of transcendental arguments have not been covered. The purpose of this Element is not to provide a comprehensive survey of this field, but to develop a polemical position that pushes the relevant debates forward. There have been many excellent introductions to transcendental arguments and epistemology. Many useful materials can already be found in those introductions, and I recommend readers to read them and compare different perspectives. This Element is not designed to replace any of them and, along the way, I have tried to avoid repetitions. As far as I can tell, the Kripkean hypothesis for transcendental conditionals has not appeared in the literature as yet, and my humble hope is that even if this hypothesis turns out to be implausible, at least we will all have learnt something important from this intellectual journey and better views can be reached by reflecting on where I went wrong in these narratives.

However, some readers might feel that this project is radically unfinished. For example, if transcendental conditions do *not* involve deductions, and they are also *not* inferences to the best explanation, then what *are* the relevant inferences? This will be the crucial question for further research. For now, I can only say this: transcendental conditionals and their rationales might *force us* to accept that certain things are of the essence of other things. For example, Kantian categories might be parts of the essence of objective cognition. If we accept the rationales for the relevant transcendental conditionals, perhaps we should say that we are *rationally obliged* to accept the relevant claims of essence. The nature of such rational obligations will be what we need to understand in follow-up projects.

References

Allen, K. (2017). Naïve Realism and the Problem of Consciousness. In H. Logue and L. Richardson, eds., *Purpose and Procedure in Philosophy of Perception*, Oxford: Oxford University Press, 43–62.

Allison, H. E. (1983). *Kant's Transcendental Idealism: An Interpretation and Defense*, New Haven, CT: Yale University Press.

Ameriks, K. (2003). *Interpreting Kant's Critiques*, Oxford: Clarendon Press.

Austin, J. L. (1961). *Philosophical Papers*, Oxford: Oxford University Press.

Bardon, A. (2006). Transcendental Arguments. *Internet Encyclopedia of Philosophy*, https://iep.utm.edu/trans-ar/.

Bell, D. (1999). Transcendental Arguments and Non-Naturalist Anti-Realism. In R. Stern, ed., *Transcendental Arguments: Problems and Prospects*, Oxford: Clarendon Press.

Bennett, J. (1979). Analytic Transcendental Arguments. In P. Bieri, R.-P. Horstmann, and L. Krüger, eds., *Transcendental Arguments and Science: Essays in Epistemology*, Berlin: Springer, 45–64.

Bermúdez, J. L. (1995). Transcendental Arguments and Psychology: The Example of O'Shaughnessy on Intentional Action. *Metaphilosophy*, 26(4), 379–401.

Bird, A. (2010). The Epistemology of Science – A Bird's-Eye View. *Synthese*, 175(S1), 5–16.

Boghossian, P. A. (2003). Blind Reasoning. *Proceedings of the Aristotelian Society Supplementary Volume*, 77(1), 225–48.

Bradley, D. (2015). *A Critical Introduction to Formal Epistemology*, London: Bloomsbury.

Bremner, J. G. (1994). *Infancy*, Hoboken, NJ: Blackwell.

Brook, A. (2001). Kant, Self-Awareness, and Self-Reference. In A. Brook and R. Devidi, eds., *Self-Reference and Self-Awareness*, Amsterdam: Johns Benjamins, 9–30.

Brueckner, A. (1984). Transcendental Arguments II. *Nous*, 18, 197–225.

Burge, T. (1996). Our Entitlement of Self Knowledge. *Proceedings of the Aristotelian Society*, 96, 91–116.

Burge, T. (2010). *Origins of Objectivity*, Oxford: Oxford University Press.

Burge, T. (2022). *Perception: First Form of Mind*, Oxford: Oxford University Press.

Byrne, A. (2001). Intentionalism Defended. *Philosophical Review*, 110(2), 199–240.

Byrne, A. and Logue, H. (eds.) (2008). *Disjunctivism: Contemporary Readings*, Cambridge, MA: MIT Press.

Campbell, J. (2002). *Reference and Consciousness*, Oxford: Oxford University Press.

Cassam, Q. (1987). Transcendental Arguments, Transcendental Synthesis and Transcendental Idealism. *Philosophical Quarterly*, 37(149), 355–78.

Cassam, Q. (1995). Introspection and Bodily Self-Ascription. In J. L. Bermúdez, N. Eilan, and A. Marcel, eds., *The Body and the Self*, Cambridge, MA: MIT Press, 311–36.

Cassam, Q. (1997). *Self and World*, Oxford: Oxford University Press.

Cassam, Q. (1998). Mind, Knowledge and Reality: Themes from Kant. *Royal Institute of Philosophy Supplement*, 43, 321–48.

Cassam, Q. (1999). Self-Directed Transcendental Arguments. In R. Stern, ed., *Transcendental Arguments: Problems and Prospects*, Oxford: Clarendon Press.

Cassam, Q. (2002). Representing Bodies. *Ratio*, 15(4), 315–34.

Cassam, Q. (2003). Can Transcendental Epistemology Be Naturalized? *Philosophy*, 78(304), 181–203.

Cassam, Q. (2005). Space and Objective Experience. In J. L. Bermúdez, ed., *Thought, Reference, and Experience: Themes from the Philosophy of Gareth Evans*, Oxford: Oxford University Press, 258–89.

Cassam, Q. (2007). *The Possibility of Knowledge*, Oxford: Oxford University Press.

Chalmers, D. J. (1996). *The Conscious Mind: In Search of a Fundamental Theory*, Oxford: Oxford University Press.

Chalmers, D. J. (2002). Does Conceivability Entail Possibility? In T. S. Gendler and J. Hawthorne, eds., *Conceivability and Possibility*, Oxford: Oxford University Press.

Cheng, T. (2018). Sense, Space, and Self, PhD dissertation, University College London.

Cheng, T. (2019). On the Very Idea of a Tactile Field, or: A Plea for Skin Space. In T. Cheng, O. Deroy, and C. Spence, eds., *Spatial Senses: Philosophy of Perception in an Age of Science*, New York: Routledge, 226–47.

Cheng, T. (2021). *John McDowell on Worldly Subjectivity: Oxford Kantianism Meets Phenomenology and Cognitive Sciences*, London: Bloomsbury Academic.

Cheng, T. (2022). Radical Internalism Meets Radical Externalism, or: Smithies' Epistemology Transcendentalised. *Asian Journal of Philosophy*, 1(1), 10.

Cheng, T. (in press). In the Transcendental Explanation of Intentionality. *Australasian Review of Philosophy*.

Cook Wilson, J. (1926). *Statement and Inference: With Other Philosophical Papers*, Oxford: Oxford University Press.

Davidson, D. (1987). Knowing One's Own Mind. *Proceedings and Addresses of the American Philosophical Association*, 60(3), 441–58.

Davidson, D. (1991). Three Varieties of Knowledge. In A. P. Griffiths, ed., *Royal Institute of Philosophy Supplement*. New York: Cambridge University Press, 153–66.

Dennett, D. (1978). *Brainstorms*, Cambridge, MA: MIT Press.

Dennett, D. (1989). *The Intentional Stance*, Cambridge, MA: MIT Press.

Dennett, D. (1991). *Consciousness Explained*, New York: Little, Brown.

Descartes, R. (1641/1993). *Meditations on First Philosophy*, D. A. Cress, trans., Indianapolis, IN: Hackett Publishing Company.

Douven, I. (2022). *The Art of Abduction*, Cambridge, MA: MIT Press.

Dray, W. H. (1957). *Laws and Explanation in History*, London: Greenwood Press.

Drayson, Z. (2012). The Uses and Abuses of the Personal/Subpersonal Distinction. *Philosophical Perspectives*, 26(1), 1–18.

Dretske, F. (1997). *Naturalizing the Mind*, Cambridge, MA: MIT Press.

Evans, G. (1980). Things without the Mind: A Commentary upon Chapter Two of Strawson's *Individuals*. In Z. van Straaten, ed., *Philosophical Subjects*, Oxford: Oxford University Press, 249–90.

Evans, G. (1982). *The Varieties of Reference*, Oxford: Oxford University Press.

Fine, K. (1994). Essence and Modality: The Second Philosophical Perspectives Lecture. *Philosophical Perspectives*, 8, 1–16.

Foote, T. (1994). Necessary Truth and the Transcendental Interpretation of Descartes's Cogito Argument. *Aporia*, 4, 1–13.

Frankish, K. (2016). Illusionism as a Theory of Consciousness. *Journal of Consciousness Studies*, 23(11–12), 11–39.

Franks, P. (1999). Transcendental Arguments, Reason, and Skepticism: Contemporary Debates and the Origins of Post-Kantianism. In R. Stern, ed., *Transcendental Arguments: Problems and Prospects*, Oxford: Clarendon Press, 111–45.

French, C. and Walters, L. (2018). The Invalidity of the Argument from Illusion. *American Philosophical Quarterly*, 4, 357–64.

Gadamer, H.-G. (1960/1989). *Truth and Method*, J. Weinsheimer and D. G. Marshall, trans., London: Continuum International Publishing Group.

Gomes, A. (2017). Perception and Reflection. *Philosophical Perspectives*, 31(1), 131–52.

Gottlieb, P. (2019). Aristotle on Non-contradiction. In E. N. Zalta, ed., *The Stanford Encyclopedia of Philosophy* (Spring 2019 edition), https://plato.stanford.edu/entries/aristotle-noncontradiction/.

Haddock, A. and Macpherson, F. (eds.) (2008). *Disjunctivism: Perception, Action, Knowledge*, New York: Oxford University Press.

Harrison, R. (1982). Transcendental Arguments and Idealism. *Royal Institute of Philosophy Lectures*, 13, 211–24.

Heidegger, M. (1927/2008). *Being and Time*, J. Macquarrie and E. Robinson, trans., New York: Harper Perennial.

Henrich, D. (1989). Kant's Notion of a Deduction and the Methodological Background of the First Critique. In E. Förster, ed., *Kant's Transcendental Deductions: The Three 'Critiques' and the 'Opus Postumum'*, Redwood City, CA: Stanford University Press, 27–46.

Hoffmann, M. H. G. (2019). Transcendental Arguments in Scientific Reasoning. *Erkenntnis*, 84(6), 1387–1407.

Hornsby, J. (1981). Which Physical Events Are Mental Events? *Proceedings of the Aristotelian Society*, 81(1), 73–92.

Hume, D. (1739/1978). *A Treatise of Human Nature*, Mineola, NY: Oxford University Press.

Husserl, E. (1913/2012). *Ideas: General Introduction to Pure Phenomenology*, W. R. Boyce Gibson, trans., New York: Routledge.

Husserl, E. (1931/1977). *Cartesian Meditations: An Introductions to Phenomenology*, D. Cairns, trans., Leiden: Martinus Nijhoff Publishers.

Hutton, J. (2019). Epistemic Normativity in Kant's 'Second Analogy'. *European Journal of Philosophy*, 27(3), 593–609.

Inkpin, A. (2016). Was Merleau-Ponty a 'Transcendental' Phenomenologist? *Continental Philosophical Review*, 50(1), 27–47.

Kannisto, T. (2020). Transcendentally Idealistic Metaphysics and Counterfactual Transcendental Arguments. In F. Kjosavik and C. Serck-Hanssen, eds., *Metametaphysics and the Sciences: Historical and Philosophical Perspectives*, New York: Routledge, 153–67.

Kant, I. (1783/1994). *Prolegomena to Any Future Metaphysics*, P. Carus, trans., New York: Pearson College Div.

Kant, I. (1787/2007). *Critique of Pure Reason*, N. Kemp Smith, trans., London: Macmillan.

Kitcher, P. (1993). *Kant's Transcendental Psychology*, Oxford: Oxford University Press.

Kornblith, H. (2021). *Scientific Epistemology: An Introduction*, Oxford: Oxford University Press.

Korsgaard, C. (1996). *The Sources of Normativity*, Cambridge: Cambridge University Press.

Korsgaard, C. (1998). Motivation, Metaphysics, and the Value of the Self: A Reply to Ginsborg, Guyer, and Schneewind. *Ethics*, 109, 49–66.

Kripke, S. A. (1980). *Naming and Necessity*, Cambridge, MA: Harvard University Press.

Kripke, S. A. (1982). *Wittgenstein Rules and Private Language: An Elementary Exposition*, Cambridge, MA: Harvard University Press.

Lewis, D. (1986). *On the Plurality of the World*, Hoboken, NJ: Wiley-Blackwell.

List, C. (2019). *Why Free Will Is Real*, Cambridge, MA: Harvard University Press.

Lowe, E. J. (2008). Two Notions of Being: Entity and Essence. *Royal Institute of Philosophy Supplement*, 62, 23–48.

Lowe, E. J. (2012). What Is the Source of Our Knowledge of Modal Truth? *Mind*, 121(484), 919–50.

McDowell, J. (1982). Criteria, Defeasibility, and Knowledge. *Proceedings of the British Academy*, 68, 455–79.

McDowell, J. (1994). The Content of Perceptual Experience. *Philosophical Quarterly*, 44(175), 190–205.

McDowell, J. (1995). Knowledge and the Internal. *Philosophy and Phenomenological Research*, 55(4), 877–93.

McDowell, J. (1996). *Mind and World*, Cambridge, MA: Harvard University Press.

McDowell, J. (1998). Having the World in View: Sellars, Kant, and Intentionality. *Journal of Philosophy*, 95(9), 431–92.

Mackie, J. L. (1965). Causes and Conditions. *American Philosophical Quarterly*, 2(4), 245–64.

Mallozzi, A., Vaidya, A., and Wallner, M. (2021). The Epistemology of Modality. In E. N. Zalta, ed., *The Stanford Encyclopedia of Philosophy* (Spring 2021 edition), https://plato.stanford.edu/Archives/spr2023/entries/modality-epistemology/.

Marr, D. (1982). *Vision*, New York: W. H. Freeman.

Martin, M. G. F. (2006). On Being Alienated. In T. S. Gendler and J. Hawthorne, eds., *Perceptual Experience*, Oxford: Oxford University Press, 354–410.

Mizrahi, M. (2017). Transcendental Arguments, Conceivability, and Global vs. Local Skepticism. *Philosophia*, 45(2), 735–49.

Moore, G. E. (1925). A Defence of Common Sense. In J. H. Muirhead, ed., *Contemporary British Philosophy* (Second Series). Sydney: Allen and Unwin.

Neuhouser, F. (1990). *Fichte's Theory of Subjectivity*, New York: Cambridge University Press.

Nozick, R. (1981). *Philosophical Explanation*, Cambridge, MA: Harvard University Press.

O'Connor, T. (2020). Emergent Properties. In E. N. Zalta, ed., *The Stanford Encyclopedia of Philosophy* (Summer 2020 edition), https://plato.stanford.edu/entries/properties-emergent/.

O'Shaughnessy, B. (1980). *The Will: A Dual Aspect Theory*, Cambridge: Cambridge University Press.

O'Shaughnessy, B. (1989). The Sense of Touch. *Australasian Journal of Philosophy*, 67(1), 37–58.

Papineau, D. (2003). Is This a Dagger? *Times Literary Supplement*, 1 December.

Peacocke, C. (1989). *Transcendental Arguments in the Theory of Content*, Oxford: Clarendon Press.

Peacocke, C. (1992). *A Study of Concepts*, Cambridge, MA: MIT Press.

Peacocke, C. (1998). Nonconceptual Content Defended. *Philosophy and Phenomenological Research*, 58(2), 381–8.

Peacocke, C. (2001). Does Perception Have a Nonconceptual Content? *Journal of Philosophy*, 98(5), 239–64.

Pereboom, D. (2022). Kant's Transcendental Arguments. In E. N. Zalta, ed., *The Stanford Encyclopedia of Philosophy* (Summer 2022 edition), https://plato.stanford.edu/entries/kant-transcendental/.

Price, H. H. (1932). *Perception*, London: Methuen Publishing.

Pritchard, H. A. (1938). The Sense-Datum Fallacy. *Proceedings of the Aristotelian Society Supplementary Volume*, 17, 1–18.

Putnam, H. (1981). *Reason, Truth, and History*, Cambridge: Cambridge University Press.

Quine, W. V. O. (1953). *From a Logical Point of View: Nine Logico-Philosophical Essays*, Cambridge, MA: Harvard University Press.

Reynolds, J. (2023). Phenomenology, Abduction, and Argument: Avoiding an Ostrich Epistemology. *Phenomenology and the Cognitive Sciences*, 22, 557–74.

Robinson, H. (1994). *Perception*, New York: Routledge.

Roca-Royes, S. (2017). Similarity and Possibility: An Epistemology of De Re Possibility for Concrete Entities. In B. Fischer and F. Leon, eds., *Modal Epistemology after Rationalism*, Berlin: Springer, 221–45.

Rorty, R. (1971). Verificationism and transcendental arguments. *Nous*, 5(1), 3–14.

Rosen, M. (1999). From Kant to Fichte: A Reply to Franks. In R. Stern, ed., *Transcendental Arguments: Problems and Prospects*, Oxford: Clarendon Press, 147–53.

Rosenthal, D. M. (2008). Consciousness and Its Function. *Neuropsychologia*, 46(3), 829–40.

Russell, M. and Reynolds, J. (2011). Transcendental Arguments about Other Minds and Intersubjectivity. *Philosophy Compass*, 6(5), 300–11.

Sartre, J.-P. (1943/2021). *Being and Nothingness*, S. Richmond, trans., New York: Washington Square Press.

Schellenberg, S. (2011). Perceptual Content Defended. *Nous*, 45(4), 714–50.

Schellenberg, S. (2018). *The Unity of Perception: Content, Consciousness, Evidence*, Oxford: Oxford University Press.

Schwenkler, J. (2012). Does Visual Spatial Awareness Require the Visual Awareness of Space? *Mind and Language*, 27(3), 308–29.

Searle, J. (1983). *Intentionality: An Essay in the Philosophy of Mind*, Cambridge: Cambridge University Press.

Shoemaker, S. (1963). *Self-Knowledge and Self-Identity*, Ithaca, NY: Cornell University Press.

Shoemaker, S. (1984). *Identity, Cause, and Mind: Philosophical Essays*, New York: Oxford University Press.

Siegel, S. (2010). *The Contents of Visual Experience*, Oxford: Oxford University Press.

Sluga, H. (1996). Wittgenstein and the Self. In H. D. Sluga and D. G. Stern, eds., *The Cambridge Companion to Wittgenstein*, Cambridge: Cambridge University Press, 320–53.

Smith, A. D. (2002). *The Problem of Perception*, Cambridge, MA: Harvard University Press.

Smithies, D. (2019). *The Epistemic Role of Consciousness*, Oxford: Oxford University Press.

Smithies, D. (2022). Replies to critics. *Asian Journal of Philosophy*, 1(1), 18.

Snowdon, P. F. (2017). The Lessons of Kant's Paralogisms. In A. Gomes and A. Stephenson, eds., *Kant and the Philosophy of Mind: Perception, Reason, and the Self*, Oxford: Oxford University Press, 245–62.

Snowdon, P. F. (2019). Strawson and Evans on Objectivity and Space. In T. Cheng, O. Deroy, and C. Spence, eds., *Spatial Senses: Philosophy of Perception in an Age of Science*, New York: Routledge, 9–30.

Sosa, E. (2007). *A Virtue Epistemology: Apt Belief and Reflective Knowledge*, Oxford: Oxford University Press.

Spiegelberg, E. (1981). *The Phenomenological Movement: A Historical Introduction*, Dordrecht: Kluwer Academic Publishers.

Stern, R. (ed.) (1999). *Transcendental Arguments: Problems and Prospects*, Oxford: Oxford University Press.

Stern, R. and Cheng, T. (2023). Transcendental Arguments. In E. N. Zalta, ed., *The Stanford Encyclopedia of Philosophy*, https://plato.stanford.edu/entries/transcendental-arguments/.

Stoljar, D. (2010). *Physicalism*, New York: Routledge

Strawson, P. F. (1959). *Individuals: An Essay in Descriptive Metaphysics*, London: Routledge.

Strawson, P. F. (1966). *The Bounds of Sense: An Essay on Kant's Critique of Pure Reason*, London: Routledge.

Stroud, B. (1968). Transcendental Arguments. *Journal of Philosophy*, 65(9), 241–56.

Stroud, B. (1999). The Goal of Transcendental Arguments. In R. Stern, ed., *Transcendental Arguments: Problems and Prospects*, Oxford: Clarendon Press, 155–72.

Stroud, B. (2011). Seeing What Is So. In J. Roessler, H. Lerman, and N. Eilan, eds., *Perception, Causation, and Objectivity*, Oxford: Oxford University Press, 92–102.

Taylor, C. (1975). *Hegel*, Cambridge: Cambridge University Press.

Travis, C. (2006). The Silence of the Senses. *Mind*, 113(449), 57–94.

Tse, C. Y. P. (2020). Transcendental Idealism and the Self-Knowledge Premise. *Journal of Transcendental Philosophy*, 1(1), 19–41.

Ward, D. (2021). Phenomenology as Radical Reflection. In H. Logue and L. Richardson, eds., *Purpose and Procedure in Philosophy of Perception*, Oxford: Oxford University Press, 234–57.

Wheeler, M. (2013). Science Fiction: Phenomenology, Naturalism and Cognitive Science. *Royal Institute of Philosophy Supplement*, 72, 135–67.

Williamson, T. (2000). *Knowledge and Its Limits*. Oxford: Oxford University Press.

Williamson, T. (2003). Understanding and Inference. *Proceedings of the Aristotelian Society Supplementary Volume*, 77(1), 225–48.

Williamson, T. (2007). *The Philosophy of Philosophy*, Oxford: Blackwell Publishing.

Williamson, T. (2013). How Deep Is the Distinction between A Priori and A Posteriori Knowledge? In A. Casullo and J. C. Thurow, eds., *The A Priori in Philosophy*, Oxford: Oxford University Press, 291–312.

Williamson, T. (2016). Modal Science. *Canadian Journal of Philosophy*, 46(4–5), 453–92.

Wittgenstein, L. (1914–1916). *Notebooks*, Chicago, IL: University of Chicago Press.

Yablo, S. (1993). Is Conceivability a Guide to Possibility? *Philosophy of Phenomenological Research*, 53(1), 1–42.

Zahavi, D. (2007). The Heidelberg School and the Limits of Reflection. In S. Heinämaa, V. Lähteenmäki, and P. Remes, eds., *Consciousness: From Perception to Reflection in the History of Philosophy*, Berlin: Springer, 267–85.

Zimmerman, A. (2010). *Moral Epistemology*, New York: Routledge.

Acknowledgements

I would like to thank Robert Stern for having me on board for the SEP entry, and Plato Tse, Cheng-Hao Lin, and Kuei-Chen Chen for participating in my seminar on transcendental arguments. I also wish to thank Quassim Cassam, Mark Kalderon, John McDowell, Rory Madden, Michael Martin, Lucy O'Brien, James Stazicker, Christopher Peacocke, and Paul Snowdon for thinking with me about many related issues. I have presented some of the materials included in this Element on various occasions, and I thank those who provided critical comments, especially Duen-Min Deng, Lok-Chi Chan, Christian Wenzel, and Dan Zahavi. Last but not least, I would like to thank Cheng-Hung Lin and Barry Stroud for showing me how good epistemology can be done. This study has been supported by National Science and Technology Council, Taiwan (NSTC 112-2410-H-004-078-MY2).

Cambridge Elements ≡

Epistemology

Stephen Hetherington

University of New South Wales, Sydney

Stephen Hetherington is Professor Emeritus of Philosophy at the University of New South Wales, Sydney. He is the author of numerous books including *Knowledge and the Gettier Problem* (Cambridge University Press, 2016), and *What Is Epistemology?* (Polity, 2019), and is the editor of, most recently, *Knowledge in Contemporary Epistemology* (with Markos Valaris: Bloomsbury, 2019), and *What the Ancients Offer to Contemporary Epistemology* (with Nicholas D. Smith: Routledge, 2020). He was the Editor-in-Chief of the *Australasian Journal of Philosophy* from 2013 until 2022.

About the Series

Epistemology is so much more than the "theory of knowledge": it is many theories, of many phenomena, still unfolding, still being tested and applied and revised and replaced. This Elements series seeks to cover all aspects of a rapidly evolving field including emerging and evolving topics such as these: fallibilism; knowing-how; self-knowledge; knowledge of morality; knowledge and injustice; formal epistemology; knowledge and religion; scientific knowledge; collective epistemology; applied epistemology; virtue epistemology; wisdom. The series will demonstrate the liveliness and diversity of the field, pointing also to new areas of investigation.

Cambridge Elements ☰

Epistemology

Elements in the Series

Foundationalism
Richard Fumerton

The Epistemic Consequences of Paradox
Bryan Frances

Coherentism
Erik J. Olsson

The A Priori *Without Magic*
Jared Warren

Defining Knowledge: Method and Metaphysics
Stephen Hetherington

Wisdom: A Skill Theory
Cheng-hung Tsai

Higher-Order Evidence and Calibrationism
Ru Ye

The Nature and Normativity of Defeat
Christoph Kelp

Philosophy, Bullshit, and Peer Review
Neil Levy

Stratified Virtue Epistemology: A Defence
J. Adam Carter

*The Skeptic and the Veridicalist: On the Difference Between Knowing
What There Is and Knowing What Things Are*
Yuval Avnur

Transcendental Epistemology
Tony Cheng

A full series listing is available at: www.cambridge.org/EEPI